Nikon Z7II User Companion

Your Indispensable Handbook with Illustrations to Master the Z7 II

By

Mats Sauer

Table of Content

INTRODUCTION

The Nikon Z7 II is a professional-grade full-frame mirrorless camera that was released in 2020. It is a successor to the Nikon Z7. The Z7 II is also compatible with the new Nikon Z MC 105mm f/2.8 VR S lens, which is a high-quality macro lens that offers stunning image quality.

The Nikon Z7 II is a versatile camera that is well-suited for a variety of photography genres, including landscape, portrait, and wildlife photography. It is also a good choice for videography, as it can record 4K video at up to 30fps.

Inside these pages, you'll find easy-to-follow instructions and clear explanations that will walk you through every aspect of your camera. From setting it up for the first time to uncovering its advanced features, we've got you covered.

No matter if you're excited to explore photography or eager to enhance your skills, this guide will help you navigate through the menus, adjust settings, and create stunning photos and videos. Get ready to unlock your creative potential with the Nikon Z7 II – let's dive in together!

Chapter 1: Getting The Camera Up and Running

Preparing the Camera for Initial Use

Setting the Language

Your camera can understand different languages and be used in different countries. It's usually set to the language of the place you're in. But if you want to change the language, follow these steps:

1. Tap on the wrench icon on the left to open the Setup Menu.
2. Find and select "Language" from the Setup Menu.

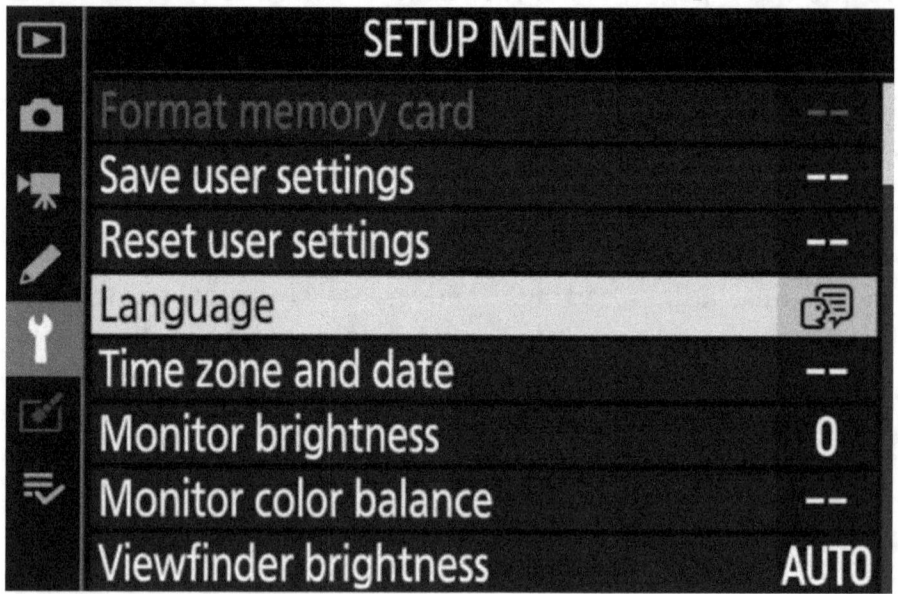

Choose the language you want, like English.

3. After that, we'll talk about the Time Zone settings.

Setting the Time Zone

Using this screen is easy as long as you know where you live. Look at the map, find your area, and choose it.

Follow these steps to pick the right time zone for where you live:

1. Go through the Setup Menu screen (Time zone and date > Time zone) until you reach the third screen.

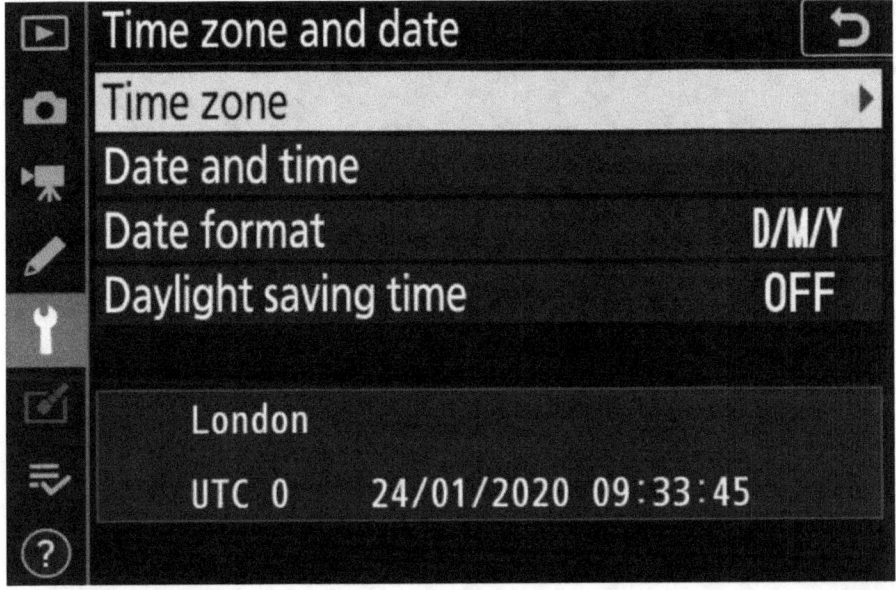

2. Use the small yellow arrows to move left and right until you find your location on the map. You'll see little yellow dots showing major cities (like New York, Toronto, and Lima) in that time zone. The city names will be above the Coordinated Universal Time number (like UTC-5). At

the bottom, you'll see the current Time zone selection. Mine is set in New York, Toronto, and Lima. Tap OK on the screen or press the OK button to confirm your Time zone.

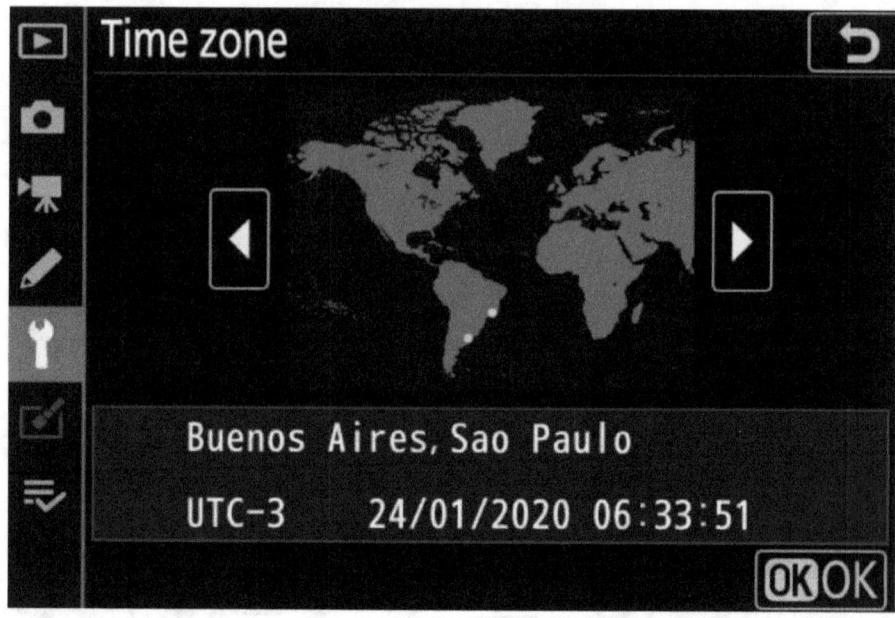

After this, you can set the Date and time settings.

Setting the Date and Time

This screen lets you put in the current date and time. The date is in year, month, day format (Y, M, D), and the time is in hour, minute, second format (H, M, S).

Here's how to set the date and time:

1. When you turn on your camera, a screen will appear on the back or viewfinder. Look for a blinking red clock

symbol. If you see this, you must set the date and time. Follow these steps (2 and 3) to do it.

2. Go to the Setup Menu and find "Time zone and date">
"Date and time." Keep following the steps until you get
to the fourth screen.

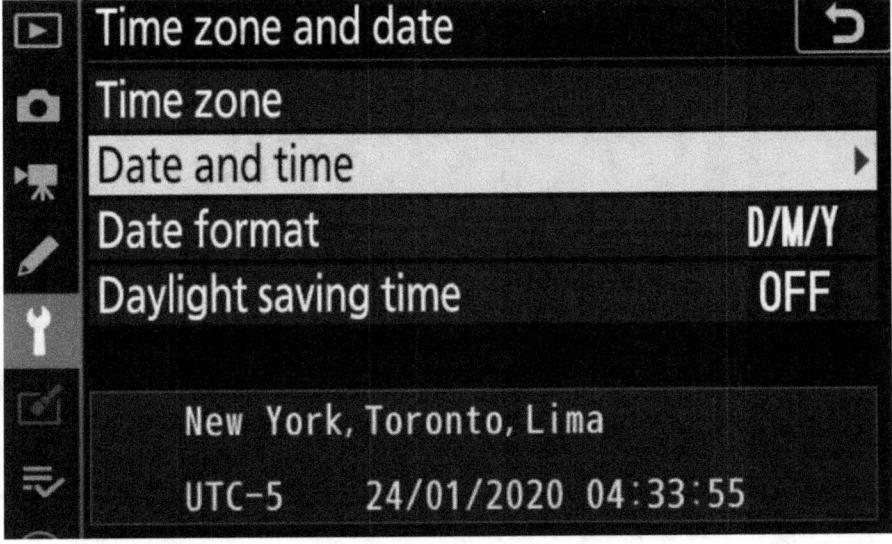

3. Choose the parts of the date and time you want to change. Use the small up or down arrows or the Multi-selector pad to adjust the values for each part (Y=year, M=month, D=day, H=hour, M=minute, S=second). The time uses a 24-hour clock, so 3:00 PM is 15:00. Press OK when you're done.

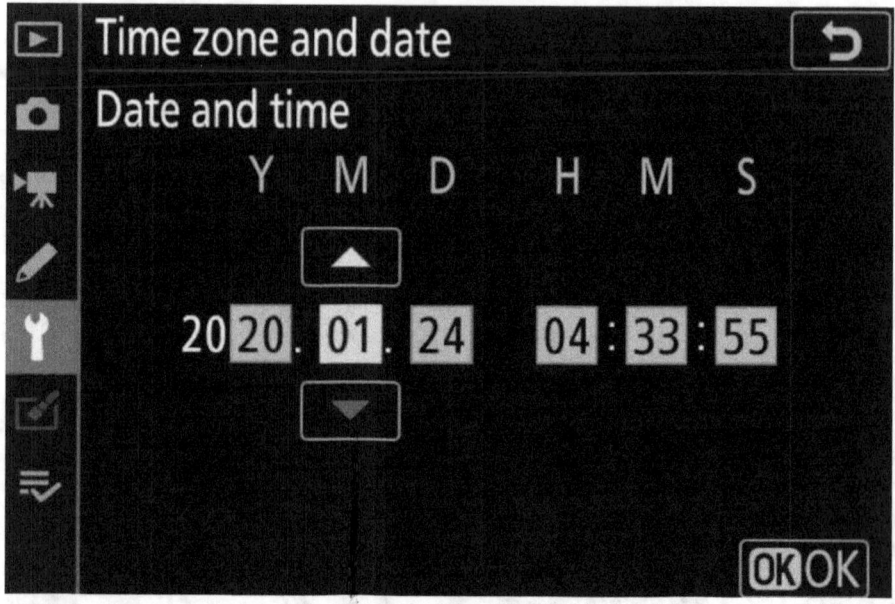

Now, let's set up the Date format.

Setting the Date Format

Different places use different ways to write dates; your Nikon camera lets you pick the one you want. There are three options:

- Year/Month/Day: 2021/01/04
- Month/Day/Year: 01/04/2021
- Day/Month/Year: 04/01/2021

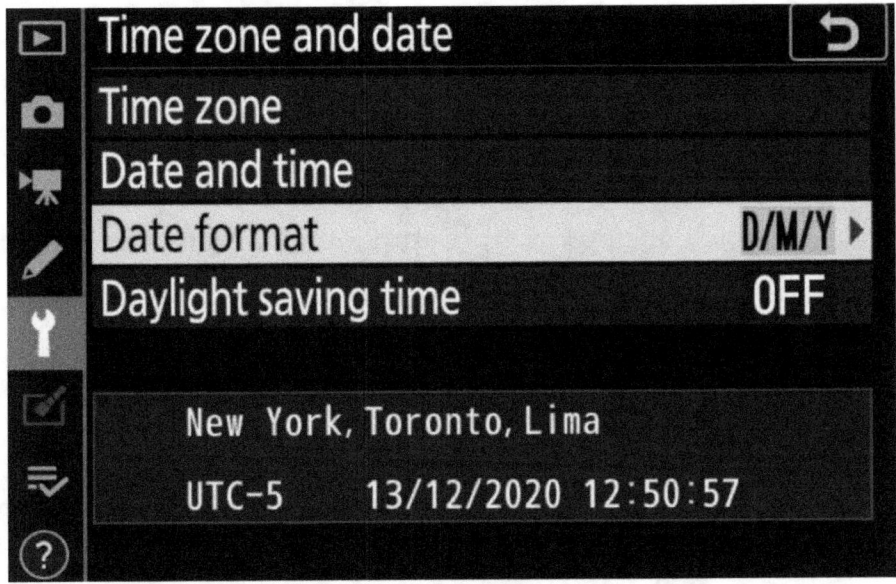

People in the United States usually choose Month/Day/Year. But you can choose the one you like. Here's how:

1. Follow the steps in the Setup Menu until you reach the third screen (Time zone and date > Date format).
2. Pick the date format you want.
3. Lastly, you can set up Daylight Saving Time if you want to.

Setting Daylight Saving Time

In some parts of the United States, we change our clocks to save daylight. During spring, we move the clocks one hour ahead, and in fall, we move them back one hour. It helps us remember the phrase "spring forward and fall back."

Your camera has a setting for daylight saving time. You can adjust your phone's clock forward or backward by an hour if daylight saving time is being followed in your area. To set this up for the first time, do the following:

1. Follow the steps on the Setup Menu screen (Time zone and date > Daylight saving time) until you reach the third screen.
2. Choose the setting you want: On or Off. If daylight saving time is happening in your area (usually in spring and summer), choose On. When daylight saving time ends, switch this setting to Off (using the Setup Menu) to move the clock back by an hour.

Exploring External Camera Features

Topside controls

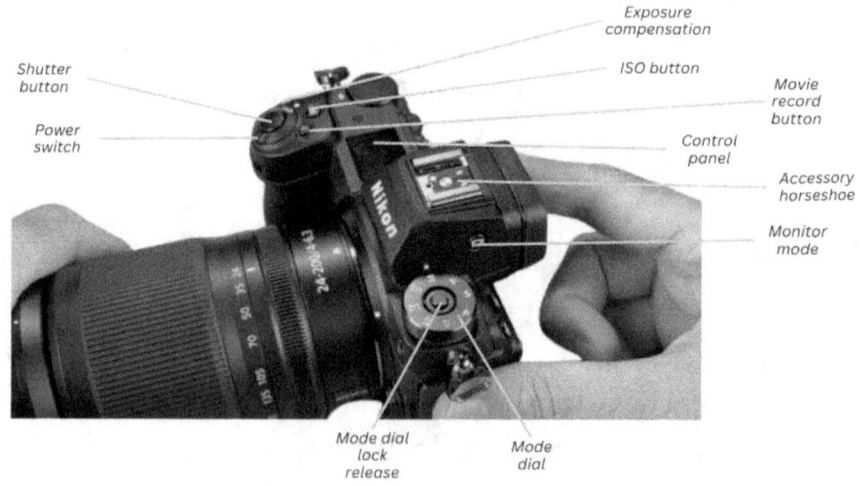

- **Mode dial:** Turn the dial to choose different shooting modes like Manual, Aperture-priority, Shutter-priority, Programmed Auto, or Auto. You can also pick user settings like U1, U2, or U3. Just unlock the dial first.

- **Mode dial lock release:** You need to press this button to unlock the mode dial before you can select any settings.

- **Accessory shoe:** Put the electronic flash into this holder for a stronger flash of light. A special flash like the Nikon SB-5000 can use the points here to talk to the camera and share things like brightness, zoom, and color info. You can also attach the Nikon GP-1a GPS adapter or Nikon ME-1 microphone here.

- **Stereo microphones:** This duo records sounds while making videos.

- **Power switch:** Turn the switch to the right to start the camera.

- **Shutter release button:** Partially press this button to turn on the exposure meter, adjust metering settings using the main and sub-command dials, and lock in the exposure and focus (unless you change the focus button). Press the button fully to take a photo. If the camera's autoexposure and autofocus turn off, tapping the shutter button brings them back. When you see a review image on the screen, tapping this button removes the image and brings back autoexposure and autofocus. You can also tap the button to leave an image review and menus, preparing the camera to take a photo.

- **Exposure compensation button:** Press and hold this button while turning the main command dial to make your pictures brighter or darker when using Program, Aperture-priority, or Shutter-priority modes. In Manual mode, the exposure doesn't change, but the suggested exposure displayed on the screen will match your adjustments. You'll see the amount of exposure adjustment displayed as a positive or negative number on the black-and-white status panel.
- **Focal plane mark:** This tool helps figure out where the sensor is pointed, useful for cases where you need to measure the distance from the sensor to the subject precisely. It is often used in scientific or close-up situations.
- **Movie button:** Tap to start recording a video and again to stop recording.
- **Control panel:** This helpful sign displays the condition of various settings.
- **ISO button:** Press and hold this button, then turn the main command dial until the ISO value you want appears on the top display, in the viewfinder, and on the monitor.
- **Speaker:** The noises from your camera come out from here.

Front-left features

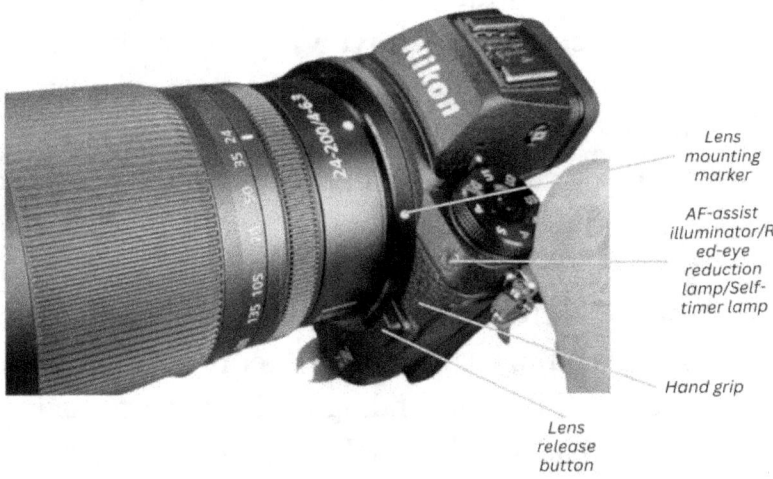

Lens
mounting
marker

AF-assist
illuminator/R
ed-eye
reduction
lamp/Self-
timer lamp

Hand grip

Lens
release
button

- **Function 1 (Fn1) button:** This button is in a good spot and does the White Balance thing when you press it. But if you change a setting, you can make it do many other things, like different ways to measure light or take a series of photos.
- **Function 2 (Fn2) button:** Normally, when you press and turn the smaller dial, the button changes the focus area. If you press and turn the bigger dial while holding the button, it changes the focus mode. You can change what this button does, just like the Fn1 button.
- **Sub-command dial:** This dial helps you change how the camera takes pictures. When there are two options to adjust together (like how much light gets in/appearance of focus), this dial changes one thing, like focus, while another dial on the back changes the other.

You can also customize how these dials work, like changing their direction or what they do.

- **Power connector cover (located** This small door can be opened to plug a cable from the AC/DC adapter into the battery compartment in the hand grip.

- **Memory card door:** Put your memory cards here by sliding the door at the back of the camera. It will open the door.

- **Shutter release button:** On the top of the hand grip, there's a button called the shutter release button. It does different things depending on how you press it. If you press it halfway, it locks the exposure and focus. Press it down to take a single photo or a series of photos if you've set it to take many. Also, if you set a timer to take photos after a delay, pressing the button will make it take 1 to 9 photos. If the exposure meters turn off, the button turns them back on. Tapping the button can also hide a menu or image on the screen.

- **On/Off switch:** Turning the switch to the marked position will switch on the camera.

- **Hand grip:** This gives you a comfy grip and holds the battery, too.

Back-of-the-body controls

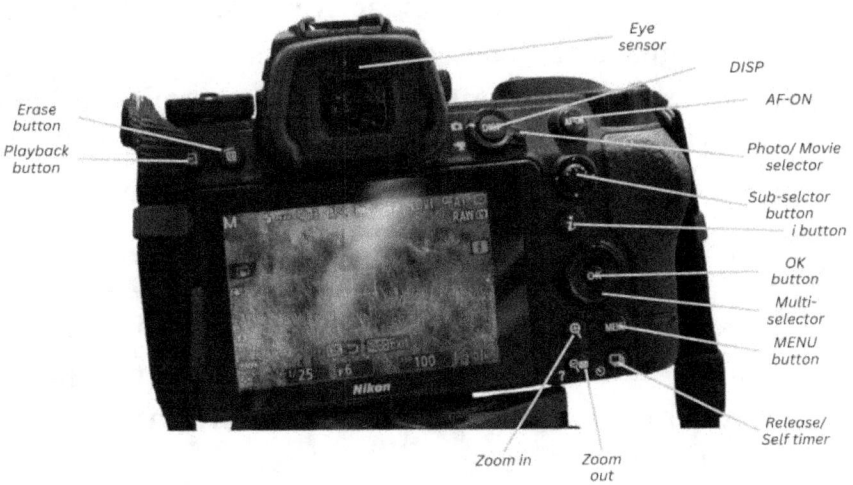

* **Playback button:** Click the button to see the pictures you've taken. I'll show you how to use the buttons and settings in the next part. To remove the pictures, press the Playback button again or tap the picture-taking button.

* **Trash button:** Tap the button to remove the picture on the screen. A message will appear on the screen, prompting you to tap the Trash button again to remove the photo or the Playback button to keep it.

* **Viewfinder eyepiece/Viewfinder window:** You can look through a clear, special viewer on the camera. It shows your picture perfectly and keeps out extra light. It has a soft edge, so it's comfortable against your eye and won't scratch your glasses. You can still see the whole picture even if you're far from it.

- **Eye sensor:** It senses when something, like your eye, gets close to the viewfinder window, usually within about three inches, based on my tests.

- **Diopter adjustment control:** First, pull the knob out. Then, turn it to fix how you see things. Push it in to keep the setting. You can make changes between -4 and +2.

- **DISP button:** Press this button to make information appear or disappear on the camera or the small screen you see. Each time you press it, the different types of information like photos, videos, and reviewing pictures will show up individually.

- **Photo/movie selector:** Changes the camera from taking pictures to recording videos. Use the AF-ON button to focus the camera without pressing the shutter halfway. This button and others let you set exposure and focus separately. To set exposure, press the shutter halfway; for focus, press the shutter halfway or use the AF-ON button.

- **Main command dial:** It is the main control dial of the camera. It's like the boss knob you use to change many things in the camera, like how fast the picture is taken, the colors, the brightness, and more. You can use it on its own or with another button. Sometimes, you use it with a smaller knob on the front of the camera. Together, they help you do things like picking picture quality (main knob: picture quality; smaller knob: sharpness), adjusting how bright the picture is (main knob: speed of picture; smaller knob: size of opening), deciding how the flash works (main knob: flash mode; smaller knob: flash strength), or fixing the colors (main knob: color setting; smaller knob: fine-tune color). You can also switch the jobs of the main and smaller knobs, change which way they turn, choose whether the lens knob or the smaller knob is used for something, and use the main knob to move around the menus and pictures.

- **Tilting LCD monitor:** The screen on the camera is 3.2 inches big and has a touch-sensitive surface. It's clear, even if you're looking at it from the side or a bit from the top, up to 170 degrees. You can see exactly what the camera sees on the screen, and it can move around. It helps you take pictures from low angles, like close-ups of flowers, or from high angles, like a periscope.

- **Charging lamp:** This light turns yellow when the camera's EN-EL15c or EN-EL-15b battery is charging with the AC adapter or another power source connected to the USB port. The light goes off when charging is done. The EN-EL15 and EN-EL15a batteries can't be charged in the camera.
  If you have the EN-EL15b or EN-EL15c batteries and want to charge them inside the camera, make sure not to turn them on when the charging adapter is connected. If you do, the battery won't charge.

- **Camera strap eyelet:** It has a little loop to attach a strap to the camera.

- **Monitor mode button:** Click the button to switch between the four LCD monitor modes. If there are modes you don't want, you can turn them off in the Setup menu under "Limit Monitor Mode Selection."

- **Automatic display switch:** It switches between the viewfinder and the monitor when your eye gets close or moves away from the eye sensor.
- **Viewfinder only:** Only shows up in the camera's view.
- **Monitor only:** Shows only on the screen.
- **Prioritize viewfinder:** The part you look through turns on and off with your eye sensor. But the screen doesn't light up when you're taking pictures. However, in the movie, playback, or menu modes, the screen does light up when you take your eye off the part you look through.
- **Sub-selector:** In the shooting mode, you can use a joystick-like control to pick where the camera focuses by moving it to the side. Pressing it down like a button will lock the focus and exposure while holding it. When looking at pictures in playback mode, the joystick acts like the regular navigation buttons to move around a zoomed-in image. You can also set it up to show the next or previous image using Custom Setting f2.
- **i button:** The button can do two things, depending on the mode.
  - **Shooting mode:** When you're taking pictures or recording videos, if you press this button, you'll bring up something called the "i menu." Inside the i menu, there are 12 different things you can change. If you don't use some things often, you can swap them out for other things you like

better. Use the "Custom Setting f1: Customize i menu."

- ○ **Playback mode:** When looking at a picture, press the i button and pick options like Rating, Select for Sending or Not Sending to a Smart Device, Retouching, Moving to another memory card, Choosing where to save, Protecting, or Unprotecting. You can choose Rating, Adjust Volume, Trim the video, Move to a different memory card, Protect, or Unprotect when watching a video. Remember, when saved on separate memory cards, the Jump to Copy on Other Card option shows a pair of images, like an original and a backup or a RAW/JPEG image.

- **Memory card access lamp:** When the lamp is on or blinking, the memory card is being used.
- **Multi-selector:** This disk, like a game controller, can move in eight directions: up, down, side to side, and diagonally. It does different things like picking a focus point, moving around a zoomed-in picture, cutting a photo, or adjusting color balance. In menus, pressing the arrows moves a cursor, the right picks an item and shows choices, and the left cancels and returns.
- **OK button:** The " OK " button in the middle of the multi-selector does different things when you press it. What it does depends on what mode you're in. You can change what it does by using a setting called Custom Setting f2.

- **MENU button:** This button makes the menu appear or disappear. This button also helps you leave a submenu and go back to the main menu when using submenus.
- **Zoom In button:** This button does two things: it helps you playback and take pictures in different modes.
  - ○ **Shooting mode:** In Shooting mode, you can press a button to make the live image look closer, which helps you focus on a specific spot. You can also move the zoomed-in view by using the directional buttons.
  - ○ **Playback mode:** Tap to make an image bigger when it's full-screen or make fewer small pictures in the index view. You can zoom in and out like on a smartphone by pinching and spreading on the touch screen. More about zooming and other playback choices in the next part.
- **Zoom Out/Index/Help button:** This button does two things: it helps you playback and shoot photos differently.
  - ○ **Shooting mode:** If you've made the picture bigger on the screen, clicking this button makes it smaller again. When you're using many choices on the menu, if you see a question mark in the corner, clicking this button shows a short help screen. This screen gives you tips on how to use the option you've selected. Using the up and down buttons, you can move through different pages on this help screen. Click this button again to go back to the menus.

- ○ **Playback mode:** Click the button to switch between full-screen and smaller views with 4, 9, or 72 thumbnails. Press the Zoom In button to return to full-screen or magnified views.
- **Release mode button:** You can pick how the camera takes pictures using the command dials. You can choose from modes like Single Picture, Continuous Low, Continuous High, Extended Continuous High, and Self-timer.

Working with Memory Cards

Inserting a Memory Card

You probably made sure your camera needs a special card to take pictures. To get ready, you need to put that card into your camera. There's a little door on the side of the camera. Slide it towards the back to open it. Ensure the camera is turned off or not busy writing on the card.

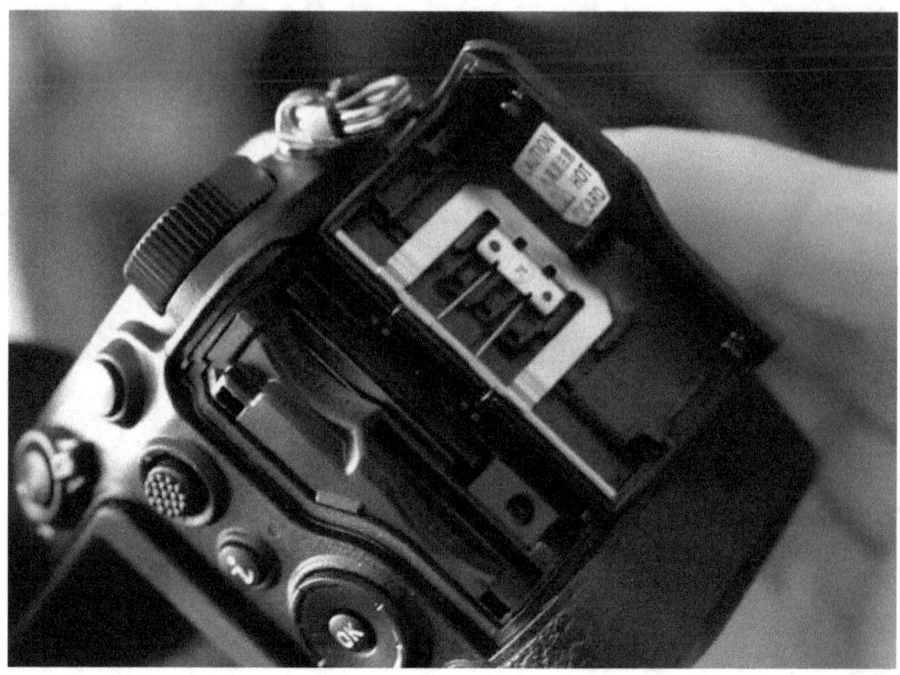

Put the card in with the writing facing the back of the camera. The part with the metal bits goes in first. Close the door, and if needed, set up the card. You can take the card out by pushing it in; it will come out a bit for you to grab.

Formatting a Memory Card

You can make an empty memory card for your camera using three methods, but only one is right. Here are the choices, with one being correct and two being incorrect:

Transfer (move) files to your computer: When you move your pictures from a camera memory card to your computer, the old pictures usually get deleted, making them empty.

However, this method doesn't delete pictures you marked as protected. It also doesn't fix parts of the card that might be broken. So, it's better to completely erase the card by formatting it when you want to start fresh. The only time you wouldn't do this is if you want to keep some protected pictures on the card for a bit longer like to show them to others.

(Don't) Format in your computer: If you want to clear your memory card and use it in your camera, don't use your computer to reformat it, even if you have Windows or Mac OS. You should put the right format on the card using the computer.

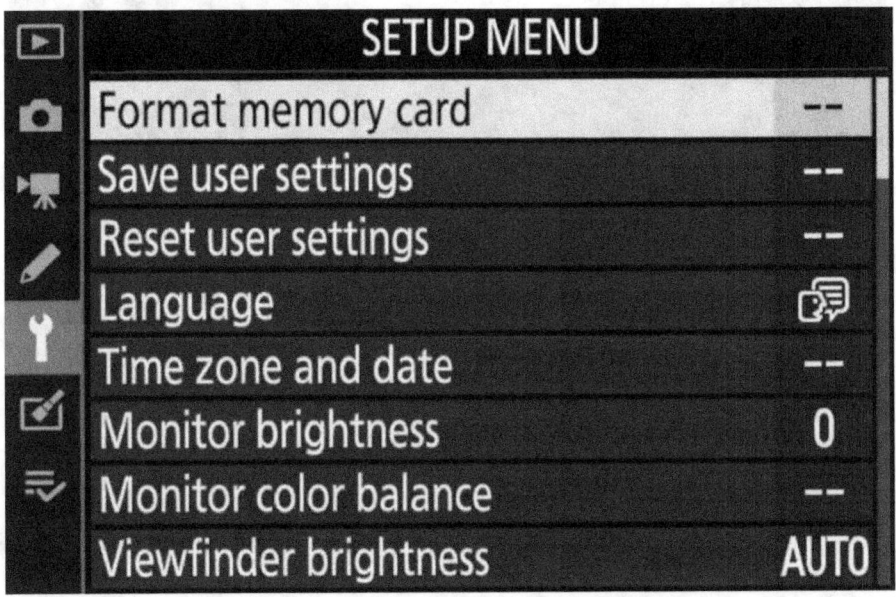

To ensure the card works well with your camera, always format it using the camera itself. You can only try formatting it on your computer if the card is messed up and the camera can't format it. Sometimes, formatting it on the computer and then trying it in the camera might help fix the card.

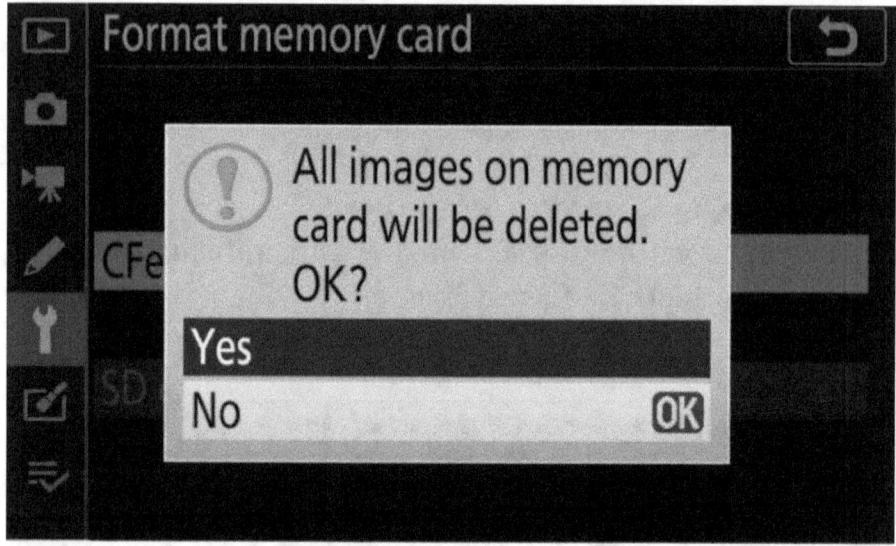

Setup menu format: To format a memory card using the recommended method, press the MENU button, use the up/down buttons to select the Setup menu (it looks like a wrench), go to Format Memory Card, choose Yes when prompted, and press OK to start formatting.

CHAPTER 2: WHITE BALANCE

Understanding the White Balance Setting

White balance is like adjusting a camera to ensure that white things look truly white and other colors look right, depending on the light where you're taking pictures. You can even use white balance to add different colors to your pictures for cool effects purposely.

Imagine the temperature scale we learn about stars, where red stars are cool, and blue/white stars are hot. The camera's white balance temperature scale works the opposite way. It adds color to fix any color problems caused by the light when taking a picture instead of giving off color based on temperature like stars do.

For example, when you're under a fluorescent light, there's not enough blue, so things might look greenish-yellow. The camera adds blue to make the picture look more normal. The white balance for many fluorescent lights is around 4000K.

Think about taking pictures on a cloudy day. The light might make the picture look bluish. Your camera's White balance control sees this and adds red to make the colors look warmer. On a cloudy day, the White balance might be around 6000K.

Just remember that we use the temperature range in reverse. Red colors are warm, and blue colors are cool. Even though this differs from what we learn in school, it's more fitting for photographers. To them, blue is cool, and red is warm. Just don't let your astronomer friends tell you otherwise.

Understanding White balance is realizing that light has colors from cool to warm. Cameras can adjust to use the light correctly or make the colors look off. This chapter explains how the Z7 II camera handles White balance.

Adjusting the White Balance setting

There are three ways to adjust the color balance on a Nikon Z camera. Let's talk about each of them.

WB on the i Menu: To easily change the White Balance settings, press the i button and choose White Balance from the menu. Ensure you're in the right Photo or Movie mode, as you can use different WB settings for photos and videos.

WB on the Photo and Movie Shooting Menus: The White balance settings on the Photo Shooting Menu change how pictures look, and the WB settings on the Movie Shooting Menu do the same for videos. These menus primarily work the same way, but there's a slight difference we'll talk about. You can use different WB settings for photos and videos.

Assigning White Balance to a camera button If you often change the White balance, you can set a camera button like Fn1 or Fn2 to control it. When you want to adjust the White balance for photos, put the Photo/movie selector on Photo mode. For videos, use Movie mode.

White Balance on the i Menu

Most photographers and videographers use the camera's i Menu to pick the right White Balance setting for their photos and videos. It is because the White Balance option is easy to find there. Let's see how to use the i Menu to choose the right White Balance:

Follow these steps to pick a White Balance setting:

1. With your subject on the screen, press the i button to open the i Menu. Choose White Balance from the bottom row, the first one on the left, and press OK or touch the WB option.
2. Pick one of the White Balance settings (like Direct sunlight) and press OK (either the button or on the screen) to finish. If you want to adjust the White Balance color more precisely, you can highlight a White Balance setting by pressing down on the Multi-selector pad or touching Adjust.
3. To adjust how colors look in your photos, you can use four color options: green, amber, magenta, and blue. There's a black square you can move towards these color options or between them. As you move the square, the colors on your subject will change. When you're happy with how it looks, press OK to finish.
4. There are also four other color choices: Auto, Fluorescent, K, and PRE. Let's learn how to use these options.

29

Auto White Balance on the i Menu

The Auto WB setting has a special screen where you can pick and adjust one of three Auto WB options (A0, A1, or A2). Let's try this out (make sure the lens cap is on for better screen contrast).

Follow these steps to choose or adjust one of the three Auto WB options:

1. Press the i button to open the i, Menu when your subject is on the screen. Choose the first option on the bottom row, the one on the left that says White Balance, then press OK or touch the WB option.
2. Look for the Auto WB choice on the left, press OK, or touch it (like A1) to keep the current Auto WB setting. If you want a different Auto WB option, scroll down using the buttons or touch the Details control. On the next screen, you can pick one of the three WB values (A0, A1, or A2).
3. Choose one of the three settings for the White Balance: A0 to make colors less warm, A1 to keep the overall feeling, or A2 to keep warm colors.
    If you want to adjust the White Balance further, pick one of the settings above and press down on the pad or touch "Adjust."

4. To make small changes to the White Balance, use four color options: green, amber, magenta, and blue. Move the black square towards a color or between two colors.

You'll see the subject's color change as you move the square. When you're happy with the changes, press or touch "OK."

Fluorescent White Balance on the i Menu

The Fluorescent WB setting has a special screen where you can pick and adjust one of seven types of fluorescent light options.

Here's how you can choose or adjust a Fluorescent WB type:

1. Look at your subject on the screen, then press the "i" button to open the "i Menu." Select the first option on the bottom row, White Balance, and press OK or touch it.
2. Find the Fluorescent WB option (for example, number 4) and press OK or touch it. If you want to try a different Fluorescent WB setting, use the buttons or touch controls to move down. It will take you to another screen to pick from the seven available options.
3. Choose one of these seven options for Fluorescent White Balance: Sodium-vapor lamps (1), Warm-white fluorescent (2), White fluorescent (3), Cool-white fluorescent (4), Day white fluorescent (5), Daylight fluorescent (6), or High-temperature mercury-vapor (7). If you want to adjust the color setting, pick a Fluorescent White Balance option and use the Multi-selector pad or touch Adjust.
4. To tweak the current Fluorescent White Balance, you have four color choices: green (G), amber (A), magenta

(M), and blue (B). Move the small black square towards a color or between two colors. The subject's color will change as you move the square. Press or touch OK to finish once you're happy with the adjustment.

White Balance Bracketing

When you use white balance bracketing, the camera takes just one photo instead of three. This first photo is always in RAW format, regardless of whether you're using JPEG, RAW, or both. If you're in JPEG mode, the camera changes the initial RAW photo into a JPEG using your chosen settings and removes the RAW version. In RAW mode, the camera keeps the RAW photo as an NEF file and makes a basic JPEG version of the picture to show on the camera screen. This small image is what you see when you check your pictures on the camera. The RAW file is seen when you put it into your photo editor. If you save in both RAW and JPEG, you get two files: the NEF RAW file (with a hidden JPEG image inside) and a separate JPEG file at the quality you want (Fine, Normal, or Basic).

When you take a picture with your camera, it captures a lot of information. If you want to take pictures with different color balances, you can tell the camera to do that. It will take one picture and then create two or three different versions of that picture with the colors adjusted. It is convenient. But remember, this only works for pictures that are saved as JPEG files, not for RAW or RAW+JPEG. The original RAW files stay unchanged and will only adjust their colors when you open them in an image editor later.

White balance bracketing changes the colors in your pictures, but it is not like exposure bracketing. Instead of f/stops, it uses "mireds" to adjust color temperature. You don't need to know much about mireds; each shot in the bracket set changes the color temperature by 5 mireds. It only affects the amber-blue colors, not the green-magenta ones.

To turn on White Balance bracketing, do these things:

1. If you're using JPEG, pick JPEG in the Photo Shooting menu's Image Quality setting.
2. Go to the Auto Bracketing setting in the Photo Shooting menu and choose WB Bracketing.
3. On the Auto Bracketing screen, after you pick WB Bracketing, scroll down to Number of Shots and pick how many sets of pictures you want with different White Balance. You have two options to choose from.
   - Choose 0, 3, 5, 7, or 9 shots using the right button. The camera will take the chosen number of pictures. They'll be evenly spread on both sides of the center point on the amber-blue scale. For instance, if you pick 5 shots, you'll get one normal picture and two, each with a bit more amber and blue. If you go for 0 shots, there won't be any extra pictures taken, just like when you turn off exposure adjustments.
   - You can select biases like B2, A2, B3, or A3 using the left button. The camera will then take two or three pictures with biases towards the blue or amber. For example, choosing B3 means you'll

get shots with increasing blue bias: a little, then a bit more, and then even more blue.

CHAPTER 3: CHOOSING BASIC PICTURE SETTINGS

Selecting an Exposure Mode

In 1980, I got my first serious Nikon camera, the Nikon FM. I remember it well because that's when I started taking photography seriously to earn money. It's surprising how much time has passed since I bought that FM! Things were simpler back then. The FM had a basic light meter, a manual exposure dial, and aperture settings. I had to decide everything about the picture. It only had one mode: M, or manual.

Later, I got a Nikon FE camera and was excited to use its A mode, which stands for Aperture-priority auto. I could choose the aperture in this mode, and the camera would determine the right shutter speed. It felt like a luxury! The FE had two modes: Manual (M) and Aperture priority (A).

After a few more years, I got a Nikon F4 camera that was more advanced and had many features. It had four modes: Manual (M), Aperture priority (A), Shutter priority (S), and Programmed auto (P). I had to learn how to use these new modes. The F4 was my first camera with all these options. Does this sound like how you've progressed? If you're older than 50, it might be familiar. If you're new to digital photography with a Nikon, I should stop reminiscing and get to the main point.

Cameras today are much more advanced than ones from a few years ago. We'll see how you can use their flexibility to your advantage. The Nikon Z7 II camera also has different shooting modes like P, S, A, and M. These modes let you control how fast the picture is taken and how much light comes in. There's also an AUTO mode for easy picture-taking when you don't want to worry about settings. We'll look at each mode closely.

To switch between modes like AUTO, P, S, A, M, and user modes (U1, U2, U3), there's a special control on the camera called the Mode dial. Let's go over each mode in detail.

Programmed Auto (P) Mode

The Programmed auto (P) mode is like a "just point and shoot" mode for taking pictures. The camera handles your settings, but you can change things if necessary. It tries to make the best pictures without you needing to do much. You can adjust the aperture by using the rear Main command dial.

P mode started as a basic AUTO mode on older Nikon film cameras. It's still on the mode dial for people who got used to it with film cameras. But even the User's Manual refers to it as a "snapshot" mode. P mode works fine in many situations, like parties, where you want to take nice, quick photos without worrying about settings. It could be better for essential photos, though. You can think of P mode as "Party" mode because it's suitable for parties!

This mode is handy when you want the camera to handle the aperture and shutter but still want control over other settings. It's similar to AUTO mode, but you can change ISO and choose when to use Flash. You can set a smaller aperture if you need a broader focus range. You control this by turning the dial, which lets you manage the aperture while the camera manages the shutter.

P mode has two parts: Programmed auto and Flexible program. The flexible program works like Aperture-priority auto (A) mode. Let me explain with an example.

Shutter-Priority Auto (S) Mode

Shutter-priority auto (S) is when you decide how fast the camera takes a picture, but the camera makes sure the lighting looks good by adjusting the aperture. If things are moving fast, like in sports or when a bird is flying, you'll want the camera to take the picture quickly so it doesn't look blurry. But sometimes, a tiny bit of blur can make the bird's wings look nice while keeping its body clear.

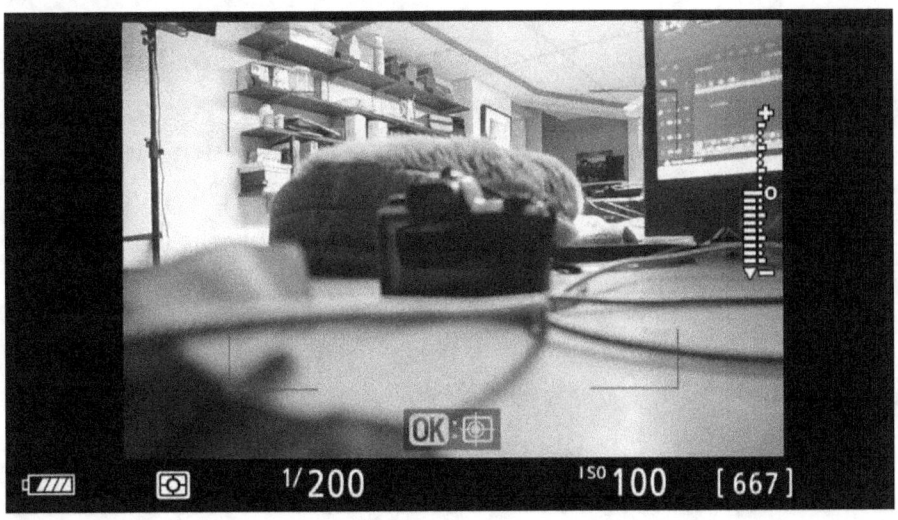

Sometimes, you can use a slow shutter speed to create special effects, like capturing a beautiful stream with a small waterfall. If the lighting changes significantly and your current shutter speed doesn't work well, the camera will show you by blinking the aperture setting. It will also display if the photo is too dark (underexposed) or too bright (overexposed) on the screen.

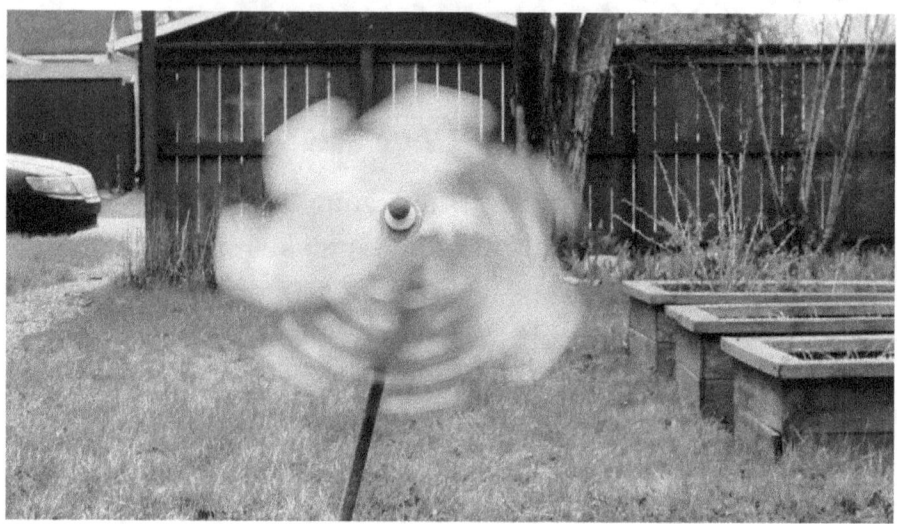

To change the shutter speed, turn the back dial on the camera to set a time between 30 seconds and 1/8000 second (or even as slow as 900 seconds with a special setting). Turn the dial left for faster speeds and right for slower speeds. The camera will try to adjust the settings for a good photo, but if it can't, it will let you know by blinking.

Aperture-Priority Auto (A) Mode

People who enjoy taking pictures of nature or close-up shots and want to control how much of the photo is in focus often use a camera setting called Aperture-priority auto mode (A-mode). This setting lets you choose the aperture (how wide the camera's opening is) while it picks the right shutter speed for a good picture. You can use the front dial on the camera to pick an aperture. Turn it one way for smaller openings (less light) and the other for larger openings (more light).

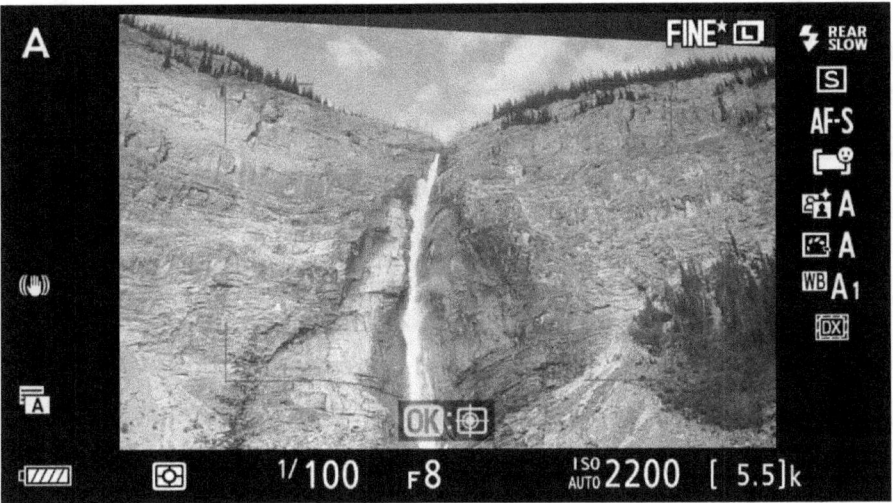

The smallest and biggest holes that the lens can make to let in light decide the lowest and highest aperture settings. Regular lenses for everyday use usually have settings from a small number like f/3.5 to a bigger number like f/22. Some more expensive lenses used by professionals can have really big holes like f/0.95 (for example, the Nikkor Z 58mm f/0.95 S lens), while zoom lenses used by pros often start at f/2.8 and go up to around f/22–f/32 (for example, the Nikkor Z 24–70mm f/2.8 S lens).

Some Nikkor S lenses have a maximum aperture of f/4, making them smaller and lighter. It helps them create obvious and sharp pictures and videos without distortion. For example, lenses like Nikkor Z 24-70mm f/4 S and Nikkor Z 14-30mm f/4 S are like this. These smaller lenses work well with the small and light Z-camera bodies.

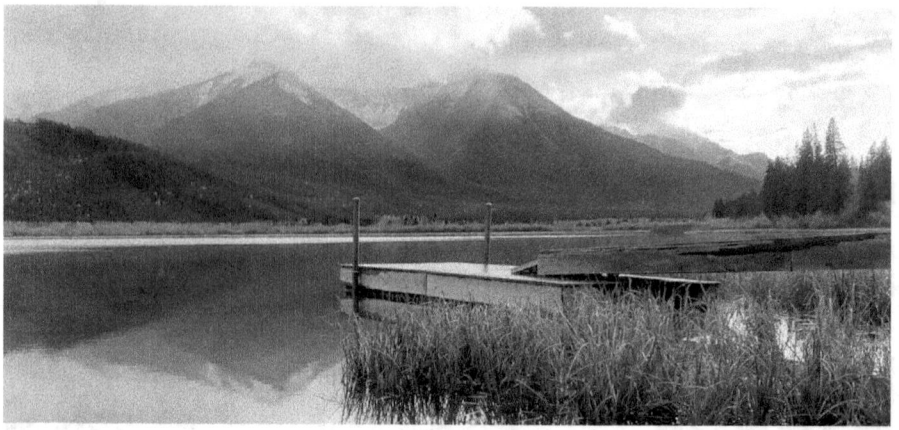

The aperture is like a control for how much of your picture is in sharp focus. It is essential for photographers. It lets you decide how much of your picture is clear and sharp.

Manual (M) Mode

Manual mode lets you decide how bright or dark your photo will be by giving you control over the camera settings. You can set the size of the hole that lets in light (aperture) and how quickly the camera takes the photo (shutter speed). There's a dial on the camera that you can turn to select Manual mode.

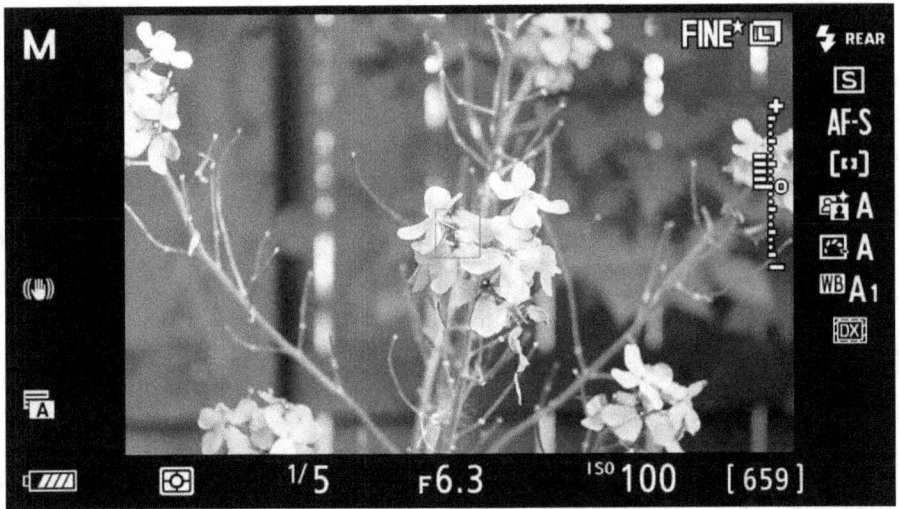

To change the amount of background blur in your photo, use the front dial. To capture motion or freeze action, use the back dial to change how fast the camera takes the picture. In Manual mode, you're the boss of how blurry or sharp your photo is and how much motion is captured. If you want the background more in focus, make the hole smaller (aperture), but also slow down how quickly the picture is taken (shutter speed) to get the right amount of light. If you need the picture taken quickly, speed up the shutter but open the hole wider to let in enough light. The camera will give you suggestions, but you can decide how bright or dark the picture should be.

The electronic analog exposure indicator appears in the viewfinder, monitor screen, or information display. It has a minus sign (-) on one side and a plus sign (+) on the other. The dots on the scale show smaller changes (1/3 of a stop), and the lines represent bigger changes (1 stop). In image 2, the indicator shows that the exposure is too bright by one stop (+1

EV), while in image 3, the indicator shows that the exposure is too dark by one stop (-1 EV).

You can adjust how sensitive this scale is by going to the Custom Setting Menu, then selecting b Metering/exposure, and finally, b1 EV steps for exposure control. You can set Custom setting b1 to either 1/3 of a stop or 1/2 of a stop. By default, the camera is set to 1/3 of a stop.

When setting the right brightness for your photo, a dashed line will show up next to a bar on the screen. On some screens, this bar appears horizontally (like a line going left and right); on others, it's vertical (like a line going up and down). This dashed line helps you see if the photo will be too bright or dark. The dashes on the line go from the middle to one side, showing if the photo is too bright or dark. You can tell how much it's off by counting the dots and lines the dashed line crosses as it moves to one side.

In Manual mode, you aim to eliminate the small bars next to or below the exposure indicator. Ensure no bars are on either side of the zero point to get the right brightness. Manual mode lets you take your time with photography. You control the picture's appearance but require more knowledge for correct brightness.

Release Modes

In the old days of film cameras, the Release modes would have been called motor-drive settings. They're about how quickly the camera can take pictures.

These Release modes are for taking photos, not videos. There are five main modes when your camera is set to Photo mode:

1. Take one picture at a time.
2. Keep taking pictures at a normal speed.
3. Keep taking pictures at a faster speed.
4. Keep taking pictures at an even faster speed.
5. Use a timer to take a picture after a delay.

However, even in Movie mode, you can take low-quality wide pictures. You can do this before or while recording a video. In Movie mode, there are two Release modes:

1. Take one picture at a time.
2. Keep taking pictures one after another.

First, ensure the camera's switch for taking photos or recording videos is set to the right mode (either Photo or Movie). Then, press the Release mode button.

After that, you'll see a screen where you can choose how you want to take pictures (Photo mode) or record videos (Movie mode). To pick the way you want to take pictures or videos, use the buttons on the camera or touch the screen. If you see a small arrow under a way of taking pictures or videos, you can press the buttons to see more options for that mode. It only works for Continuous L and Self-timer modes, which have more settings. Remember how to do this because we'll talk about these options later.

You can know which Release mode you're using (like S, L, H, H*) by looking at the bottom-left part of the Control panel on the camera without going into the menus.

Now, let's explore each Release mode more closely to understand how they can assist you in taking good pictures. The Release mode screens are shown with the lens cap on to provide clear differences.

Single Frame

The Single Frame Release mode is the most straightforward setting. It takes one picture when you press the picture-taking button. There are different modes for taking photos and videos, and Single Frame is the first one. To choose it, press the mode button and select Single Frame from the screen. This mode is for taking one picture at a time and only works slowly like some other modes.

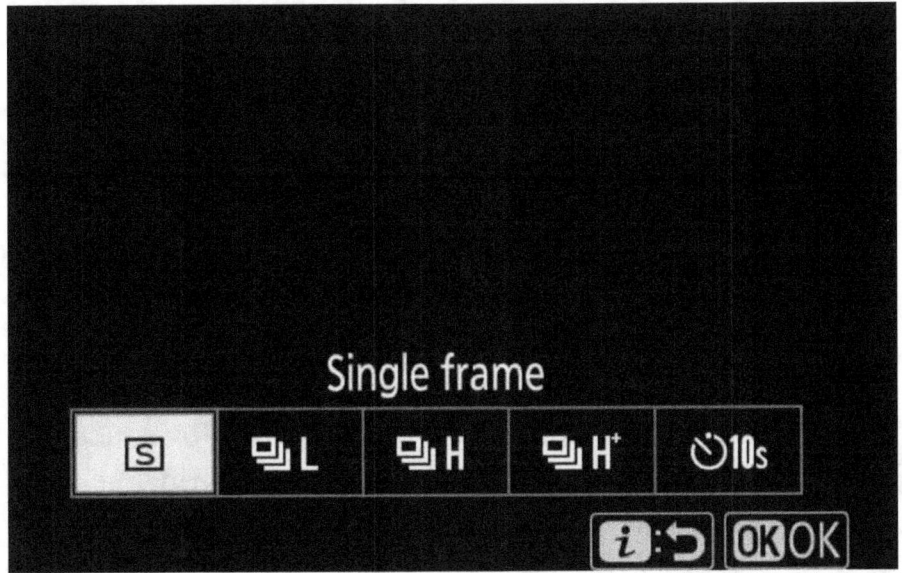

Nature photographers often use this mode because they care more about getting the right focus and a great arrangement in their photos than capturing lots of pictures quickly. This mode is also good for taking pictures of people, like in portraits, graduations, weddings, and events. You get one picture each time you press the picture-taking button.

When the camera is set to Movie mode, the Single Frame Release mode lets you take a single picture in the same shape as a widescreen movie (16x9). This picture's size and shape match what's set for the movie mode. You can take one picture when you're not recording a video. But if you're recording a video, pressing the picture-taking button down captures one picture from the video without stopping the video itself. You can take up to 50 pictures while recording one video.

Continuous (Movie mode only)

In Movie mode, there's something called Continuous Release mode. It differs from the Continuous L or Continuous H modes in Photo mode. When you're not recording a video, this mode lets you take many widescreen pictures in a row for up to three seconds by holding the picture-taking button.

To get to Continuous mode, make sure you're in Movie mode (move the lever to the lower position) and press the Release mode button. Choose Continuous mode on the Movie mode by highlighting it and pressing OK or tapping the setting.

Caution: Be extremely cautious when using the Movie mode's Continuous mode (not the Photo mode's Continuous L or H). When you're not recording a video, you can use a Single frame (taking one picture at a time) or Continuous (capturing many pictures rapidly). In Continuous mode, the camera can take hundreds of wide images in just a few seconds if you press the Shutter-release button. It's like making a short manual movie without recording video; each frame of this "movie" will become a separate picture on your camera's memory card.

Each picture here is like a single frame from a 16x9 video. A 1080p picture is around 2 million pixels big, while a 4K picture is about 8 million pixels big. The camera can only hold a certain number of pictures at once, but the card that stores them is so quick that it can instantly empty the camera. It means you can take many more pictures in a row than you might have thought. The camera stops taking pictures after three seconds to prevent too many at once. But during those three seconds, you can take hundreds of pictures. I won't say how I found this out, but you can probably guess.

When you're making a video and push the picture-taking button, the camera will capture one widescreen photo, whether you take one or multiple pictures simultaneously. It won't stop the video recording.

Continuous L

Continuous L Release mode lets you choose how fast your camera takes pictures, from one to five pictures per second. You can only use this mode when taking photos, not videos.

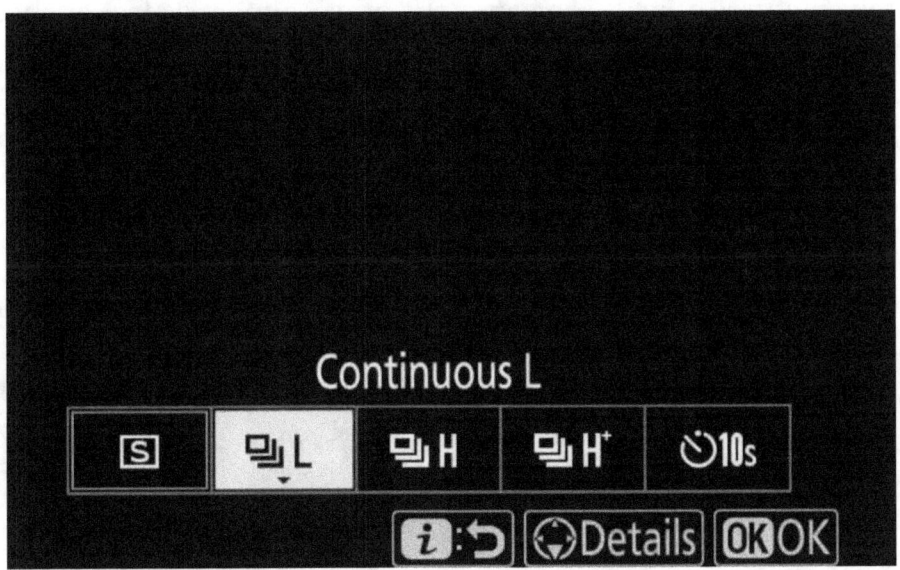

To get to this mode:

1. Press the Release mode button and select Continuous L.

2. Pick how many pictures you want the camera to take per second, from 1 to 5.

3. Press OK to finish.

When you take pictures with the camera's regular button, the screen might go black for a moment after each picture. The camera will focus and adjust the brightness for each picture automatically. If you use the quiet mode with the electronic button instead of the regular one, the number of pictures taken per second might change slightly.

Continuous H

Continuous high-speed Release mode is used when you want to take pictures quickly, one after the other, almost as fast as the camera can. This mode isn't available when recording videos. To use it, press the Release mode button to open the options, then choose "Continuous H" from the Photo mode options.

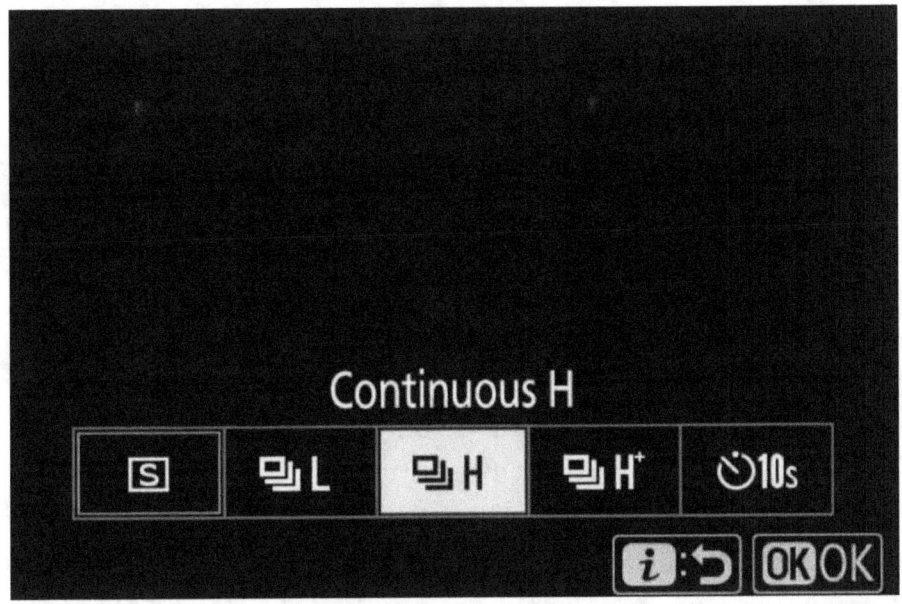

The speed of the regular shutter is 5.5 frames per second for regular and high-quality RAW photos. But if you choose the highest quality RAW photos, the speed becomes 5 frames per second. In the quiet mode with no shutter noise, the speed becomes 4 frames per second for regular and high-quality RAW photos and 3.5 frames per second for the highest-quality RAW photos.

Continuous H (Extended)

Continuous H (extended) Release mode is a super-fast mode for taking pictures. It doesn't go black when you're shooting quickly. But you can't use it for recording movies. Press the Release mode button to reach this mode and pick Continuous H (extended) from the Photo mode screen.

With the regular shutter, the camera takes 10 pictures per second in a special high-quality format. But the speed drops to 9 pictures per second if you use an even higher-quality format. In a quieter mode that doesn't make noise, the speed is 8 pictures per second for regular quality, and for the higher quality, it's 6.5 pictures per second.

Self-Timer

Use the Self-timer Release mode on your camera if you want to take pictures a few seconds after you press the button to take a photo. When you press the button halfway down, the camera will focus; if you press it down, the Self-timer will start. Remember, you can't use this mode when shooting videos.

To get to this mode, press the Release mode button. Then, choose the Self-timer Release mode and press down on the pad. You can select how long you want to wait before the camera takes the picture (2 seconds, 5 seconds, 10 seconds, or 20 seconds). You can also pick how many pictures the camera will take in this Self-timer mode (from 1 to 9 shots). When you're done deciding, press OK. By default, the Self-timer will wait for 5 seconds.

Using the Custom Setting Menu, you can change the timing before the camera takes a photo. You can set how long it waits (from 2 to 20 seconds), how many photos it takes (1 to 9 shots), and how much time between each photo (from 0.5 to 3 seconds).

If you want to hear a beep sound while the timer is counting down before taking a photo, you can adjust that in the Setup Menu under the Beep options.

Once you push the button to take a picture with the timer on, a light will blink, and a sound will start. When only two seconds are left, the light will stay on, and the sound will get faster. When the sound is super fast, your time is up, and the picture is taken. To stop the timer, press the MENU or Playback button.

Setting Resolution and File Type (The Image Quality Setting)

Considering resolution: Large, Medium, or Small?

Image size refers to how many megapixels your camera uses when taking pictures. The default setting for the Z7 II is 45.4 megapixels. You can change this by picking different sizes like FX, DX, 1:1, or 16:9. It changes how detailed the pictures are. Let's see how to do it for all five sizes.

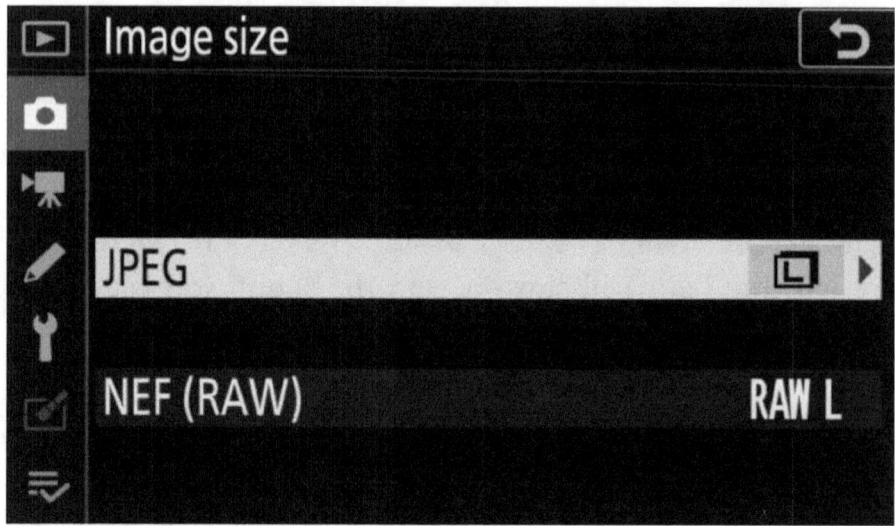

Image Size for JPEG Files

These are the steps to pick the size of a picture for JPEG images. Even if two pictures have the same detail, their file sizes will differ. JPEG images use a kind of compression that makes the file sizes smaller. Each picture size option is measured in megapixels.

The size of the picture in terms of pixels (like 6048 × 4024 or 8256 × 5504) and the megapixels (like 24.3 M or 45.4 M) will be different depending on the setting you choose for the picture area (like FX, DX, 5:4, 1:1, 16:9). This was explained a few pages ago (page 186). The numbers in this section are based on the FX picture area setting. If you change to a different picture area setting, the size values will change, too.

Image Size for NEF (RAW) Files

The camera offers three sizes for NEF (RAW) Images - Large, Medium, and Small. The picture shows the megapixel sizes for each setting, depending on your camera model. The size values of the images will change based on the Image area you previously chose (like FX or DX), and we're using the FX Image area values here.

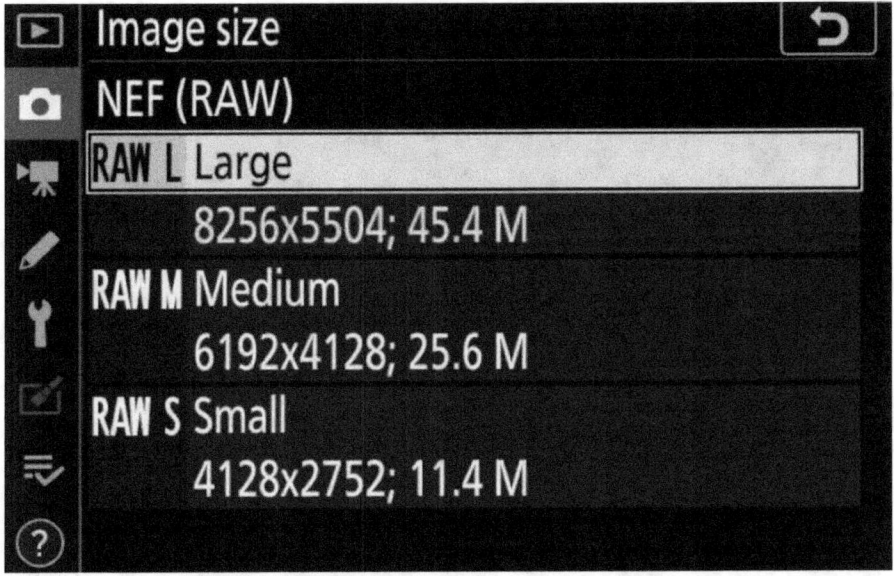

Understanding file type (JPEG or Raw)

New photographers might need help deciding which format to use for their pictures. It's a good idea to use all three formats at different times. There are 13 options, but they all come down to two types: NEF and JPEG. Let's talk about these formats briefly:

NEF (RAW): This format is for photographers who want to edit each picture after taking it. When you use RAW, the camera captures the light information but doesn't turn it into a ready-to-use picture. You need to do that on your computer. It takes more effort, but you get the best possible picture quality. You can also turn a RAW picture into a JPEG right in the camera using a function.

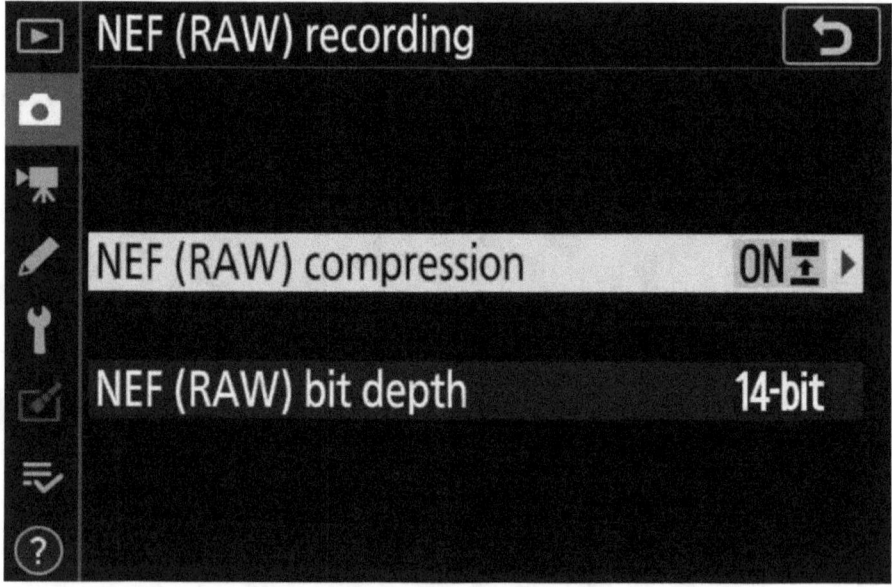

JPEG: The 8-bit JPEG format is a quick way to get a picture that's ready to use. It takes some of the extra stuff from the picture and makes it smaller so you can use it immediately. But you can change it slightly, or it might not look as good. Use JPEG when you need a picture and want to save time on it. JPEG files are smaller than RAW files, but the picture quality depends on how complex the scene is. The camera has different levels of compression for JPEG files. Some have a star symbol, which means they're better quality, while others focus more on making the file size smaller. The ones with the star have higher quality but bigger file sizes, especially for complex pictures.

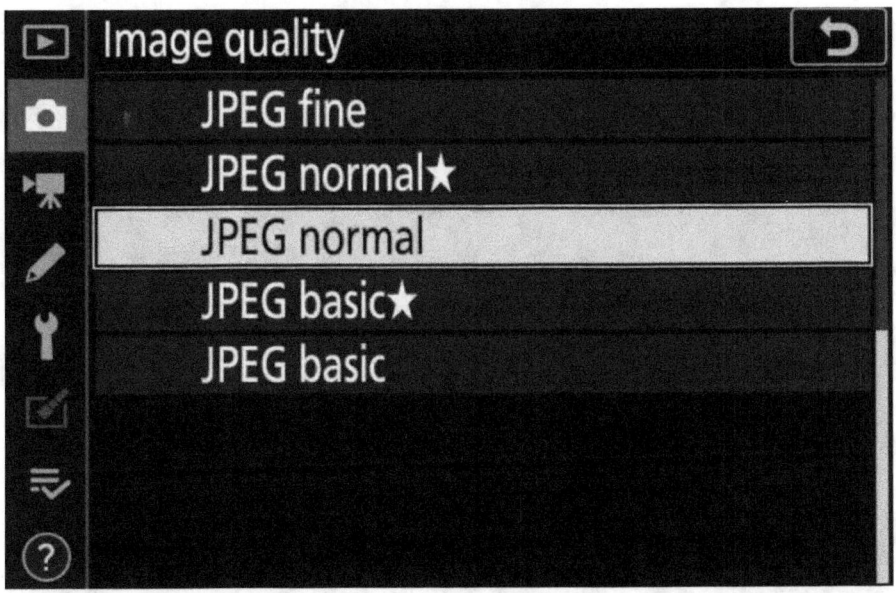

Combined NEF and JPEG Shooting (Two Images at Once): Some photographers use different settings on their camera to take two pictures at once. One picture is in a high-quality format called RAW, and the other is a regular JPEG picture. This way, they get both types of pictures when they take a photo. These settings are listed at the top of a menu on the camera, and they include options like:

- NEF (RAW) + JPEG fine*
- NEF (RAW) + JPEG fine
- NEF (RAW) + JPEG normal*
- NEF (RAW) + JPEG normal
- NEF (RAW) + JPEG basic*
- NEF (RAW) + JPEG basic

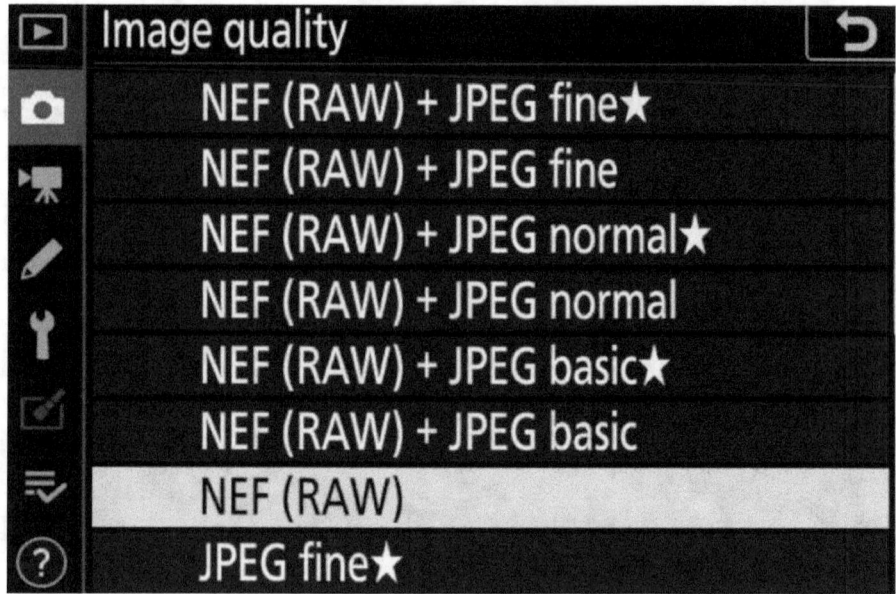

With these combined modes, you can save all the image details in an NEF (RAW) file to work on later and use a JPEG file immediately without any changes.

You don't need to know all the details about these modes because the NEF (RAW) + JPEG modes offer the same features as each mode. The RAW file in NEF (RAW) + JPEG mode is like a regular RAW file in standalone NEF (RAW) mode. The JPEG in NEF (RAW) + JPEG mode is like a regular JPEG image, whether fine, normal, or basic, without the NEF (RAW) file.

CHAPTER 4: TAKING CHARGE OF EXPOSURE

Introducing the Exposure Trio: Aperture, Shutter Speed, and ISO

Getting a Handle on Exposure

This part explains the basic ideas behind making a photo look good. You can skip to the next part if you know about f/stops, shutter speeds, and how sensitive the camera's sensor is to light.

Making a photo look right is about using light well. When a photo has the right light, you can see all the details and colors you want. But if the light is wrong, essential parts can be too dark or bright. However, making a photo look perfect can be challenging. Cameras or your skills need to figure out how to capture all the different shades and colors. Cameras can't do it perfectly like our eyes do. So, if a photo has a wide range of dark and bright parts, we often have to choose an amount of light that makes most of those shades look good, even if it doesn't capture every shade perfectly.

If you own a Z-series mirrorless camera, you probably know about the three things that affect how bright your photos are: how much light comes in through the lens (aperture), how long the camera's "eye" stays open (shutter speed), and how sensitive the camera's sensor is to light (ISO). They all work together. With more light, you can open the "eye" wider, keep it open longer, or make the sensor more sensitive. It makes your photo brighter. You can also change one of these things while changing another to keep the brightness the same.

Using any of the three camera controls comes with trade-offs. Using larger f/stops makes some parts of the image blurry while using smaller f/stops makes more of the image clear but can cause blurriness due to diffraction. Shorter shutter speeds help capture still subjects, while longer shutter speeds can make moving subjects look blurry. Higher ISO settings add graininess to the picture, while lower ISO settings reduce this graininess.

To better understand how light affects your photos, consider six factors that work together to create an image. Begin with a light source, like the sun, a lamp, a flash, or a campfire. Follow the path of light as it enters your camera, passes through the lens, and reaches the sensor that captures the picture.

Here's a quick explanation of the stuff we can control that affects how much light hits the camera sensor, listed in the order of how the light goes from the subject to the sensor.

Light at its source: Our eyes and cameras see best in visible light. This light has colors and brightness that matter in photography. When taking pictures, the brightness of the light source is essential. Sometimes, we can change the brightness ourselves, like with indoor lights or camera flashes. Other times, we can't change the brightness directly, like with sunlight. But we can make sunlight appear less bright by using materials that absorb or reflect some light.

Light's duration: We usually think of light as always being on, but sometimes, it can change quickly, like when a photo's main light comes from a flashing light, affecting how the photo looks.

Light reflected, transmitted, or emitted: After light comes from a source, like a lamp or the sun, it bounces off things and enters our camera. It is how we're able to see and take pictures. Sometimes, light goes through things like plastic or comes right out of things like a candle, and we can still see them. If a lot or a little light goes into the camera, we can change some settings to make the picture look better. We can add more light to the thing we're taking a picture of or make the light that's already there brighter.

The light passed by the lens: Not all the illumination that reaches the front of the lens makes it all the way through. Filters can remove some of the light before it enters the lens. Inside the lens barrel is a variable-sized diaphragm that produces an opening called an aperture that dilates and contracts to control the light that enters the lens. You, or the camera's autoexposure system, can control exposure by varying the size of the aperture. The relative size of the aperture is called the f/stop.

Light passing through the shutter: After light goes through the lens, the shutter decides how long the sensor gets the light. The shutter can be open quickly, like 1/8000th of a second, or it can stay open for a long time, up to 30 seconds, or even more if you choose special settings like Bulb or Time. These settings are only in Manual mode.

Light captured by the sensor: Not all the light that goes to the camera's sensor is captured. If not enough light reaches a spot on the sensor, no information is recorded. Likewise, if too much light hits a pixel on the sensor, it isn't recorded or could affect nearby pixels. We can change how much detail is in the image by adjusting the ISO setting. A higher ISO makes the sensor more sensitive by boosting the incoming light.

Four things affect how a photo looks: the amount of light, how much light the lens lets in, how long the camera's shutter is open, and how sensitive the sensor is. These factors work together so that if you change one, you must change the others to keep the photo looking right. For example, if you double the light, make the aperture larger, leave the shutter open twice as long, or double the ISO, the photo will be twice as bright. And you can make the photo less bright by doing the opposite.

But when you adjust the P, A, or S mode settings, the exposure doesn't change because the camera adjusts to keep the exposure the same. That's why Nikon offers other ways to change exposure in those modes.

Choosing a Metering Method

The camera has four different ways of looking at the light it gets through the lens: Matrix, Center-weighted, Spot, and Highlight-weighted. You can choose how you want it to look by using the i menu or setting it up yourself in the Custom Setting f2.

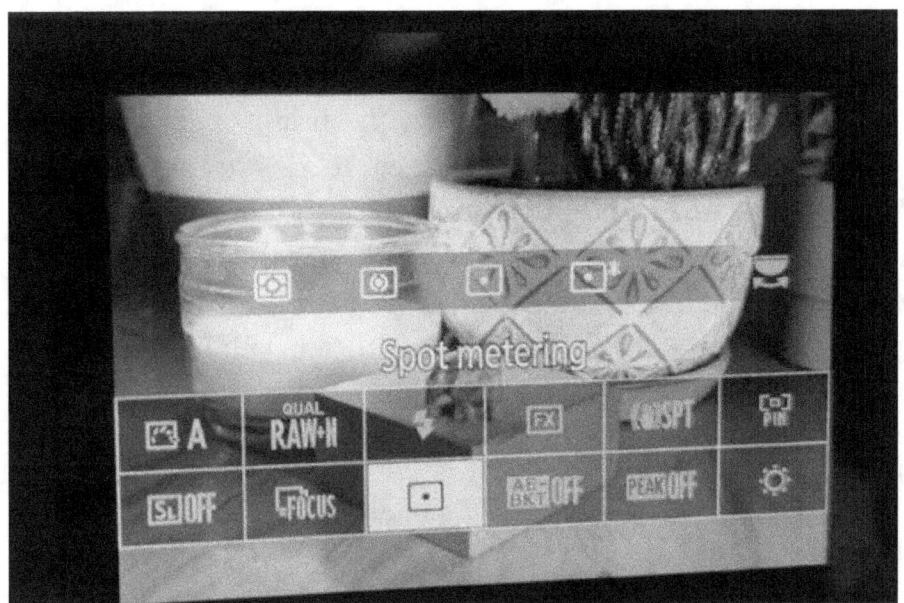

Your camera determines the right amount of light by checking how much comes through the lens and hits the sensor. The sensor can see a range of dark to bright, from very dark to very bright. Think of it like going from being outside at night with a full moon (not very bright) to a sunny day with snow (very bright). Your camera can notice a lot of different kinds of light, but it can only really take pictures in a smaller range. Remember that the sensor can detect more kinds of light than it can capture in a photo. It's easy to mix up these two different things.

Matrix Metering

In Matrix metering mode, the camera checks the light on its sensor and compares how bright different parts of the scene are using a grid. When you turn on Matrix metering, a symbol

61

shows up on the screen with photo details. You can make this appear by pressing the DISP button. Then, the camera compares the differences between the bright and dark areas with a library of 30,000 real images. It tries to make a smart guess about what kind of picture you're taking. For instance, if the top of the picture is much brighter than the bottom, the camera might think it's a landscape with a lot of sky. But if there's a bright spot in the middle with skin colors, the camera will guess it's a portrait and adjust the exposure for the person's face.

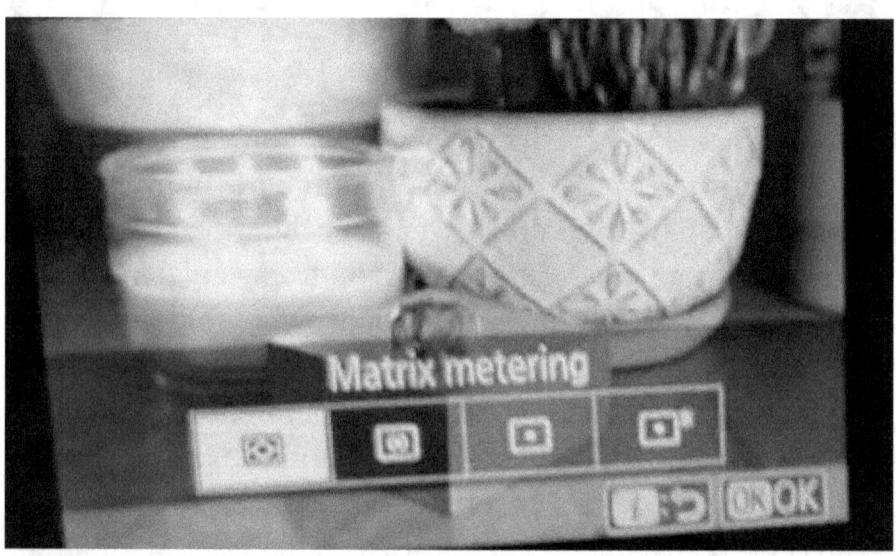

Matrix metering mode helps your camera recognize and adjust for bright situations. It makes sure your photos are light enough. It is great for snowy landscapes or close-ups of people in white clothes. Sometimes, you might need to adjust the exposure a bit, but usually, it gets it right on its own. In my experience, Matrix metering works best when sunny and bright, especially with people in the photo. But on cloudy days, it might work better and could make photos too dark.

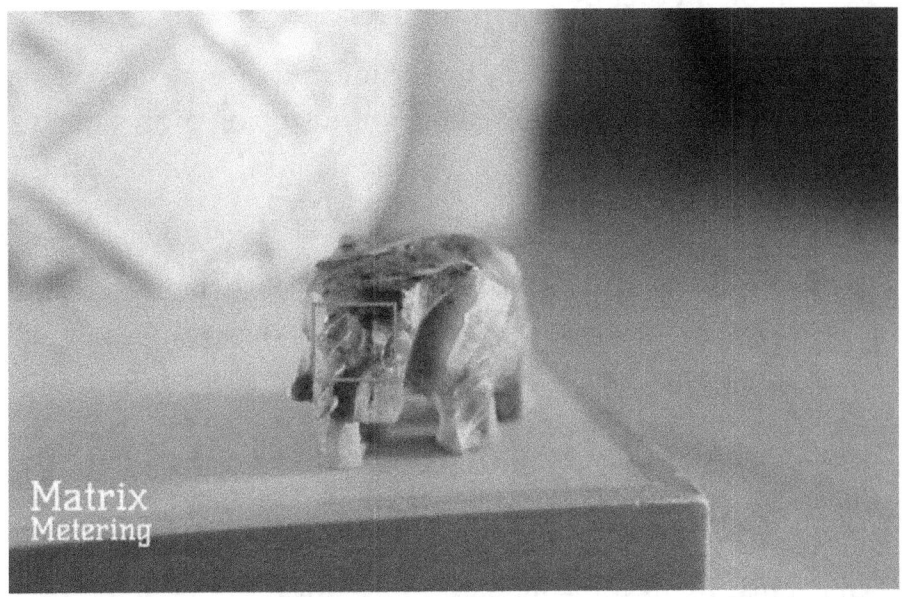

Exposure meters have always used brightness to figure out the right settings. The new exposure-meter technology uses more clever information to set things better. It includes:

Patterns: Earlier, we discussed how the camera checks the brightness of all its pixels and compares them to many different pictures it knows. It's looking for what's the same and what's different. When it finds a picture that looks like yours, it suggests how bright your picture should be.

If a picture has bright and dark parts, the camera usually focuses on the bright parts. Later, you'll discover that if the bright parts lose detail, they can't be returned. But sometimes, we can get back some details from the dark parts. If you specially take pictures, you can make the dark parts brighter and see more in them.

Colors: The camera can get better information by looking at the colors in the picture. If there's a lot of blue on top, it's probably the sky. If there are greens, it's likely plants. And if there are skin colors, it's probably people.

Autofocus area: If you or the camera picks where to focus, the exposure system thinks that whatever is sharp in the picture is what you want to capture.

Distance and focal length: The Z-mount lenses help the camera figure out what kind of picture you're taking. If you're using a lens that makes faraway things look bigger, and you're taking a picture of someone 5 to 12 feet away, and the top part of the picture is bright, the camera thinks you want the rest of the picture to look good and will ignore the bright part. But if you're using a lens that shows a wide view and you're focused on things far away, the camera thinks you're taking a picture of a wide scene like a landscape, and it will make sure the bright top part of the picture, like the sky and clouds, looks good too.

Matrix metering is a good choice for most regular pictures. It looks at the scene and can usually guess what you're taking a picture of. It knows if the things in the picture are very different in brightness. It helps the camera decide how bright or dark the picture should be. Sometimes, when the picture has bright and dark parts, the camera might make it a little darker to keep the bright parts from becoming white. It is essential because you can usually fix dark parts later, but once the bright parts turn white, you can't fix them.

Center-weighted Metering

In this mode, the camera focuses on a small area in the center of the picture to decide how bright the photo should be. This way of measuring light used to be the only choice a long time ago and was seen as an improvement from another way that just looked at the overall brightness of the whole picture.

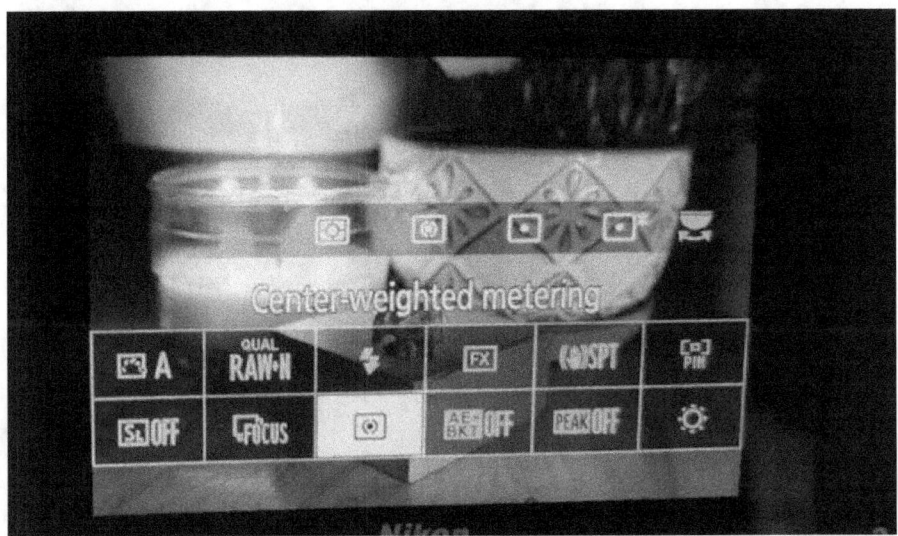

When you use Center-weighted metering, the camera doesn't understand the scene like a smart person would. It looks at the brightness all over the picture but pays extra attention to the middle part. It is because the main thing you're taking a picture of is usually somewhere near the middle.

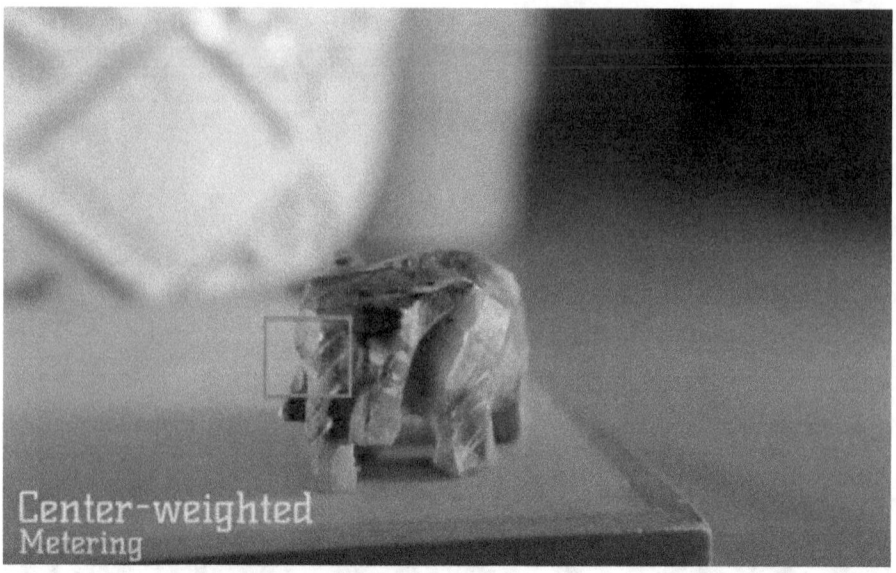

Center-weighted
Metering

About 75% of the camera's attention is focused on the center part of the image, while the remaining 25% considers the rest of the picture. Suppose the camera decides that the middle area needs an exposure f/4 at 1/250th of a second, and the outer area is darker, needing f/16 at 1/250th of a second. In that case, the camera gives more importance to the center and sets the final exposure to something like f/5.6 at 1/250th of a second.

This method works best when the main subject in the middle is a normal brightness. But if your subject is in the center and there are a lot of really bright or very dark areas around it, the exposure might need improvement. In those cases, you could use exposure compensation to fix it. However, this method works well when using only one mode for close-up shots of flowers or portraits. Adjusting the settings, you can change how much attention the camera gives to the center. The default 12mm circle works fine in most cases.

Spot Metering

Spot metering is a mode in your camera that's helpful if you've used a separate device to measure light in different parts of your photo, like the bright and dark areas. But you can also use Spot metering to measure the light in small sections of your subject, whether bright, medium, or dark.

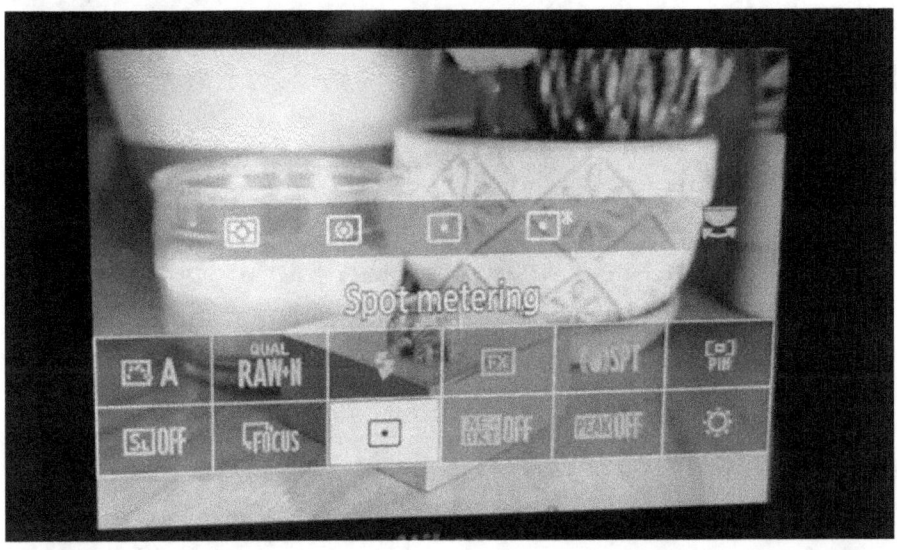

In this mode, the camera measures light in a tiny 4mm spot, only about 1.5% of the picture. You'll see a blue circle that shows where this spot is. It's right in the middle of the area you're focusing on but a bit bigger than the focus point. So, remember that it's not just measuring light where the focus point is. It is the only way to choose exactly where to measure light in your photo. However, if you're using Auto-area AF, the camera only uses the center focus point for spot metering.

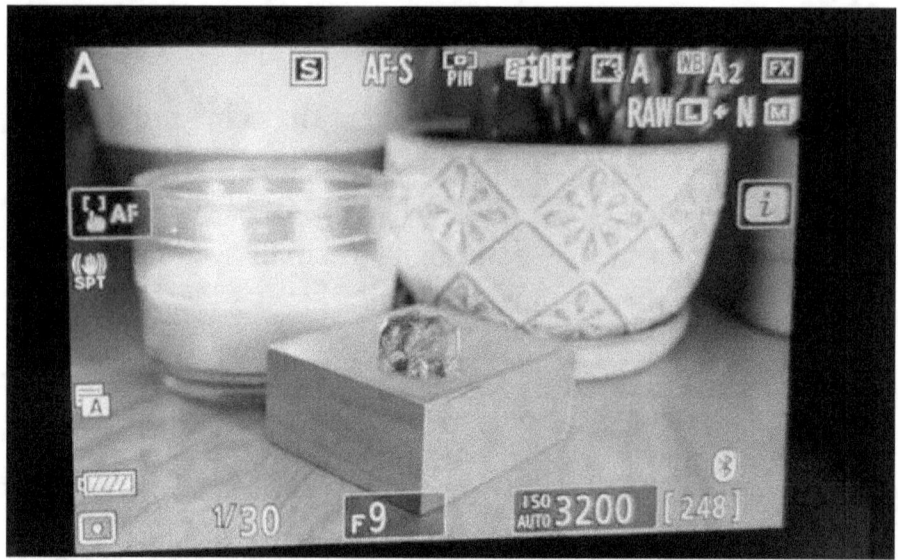

Spot metering is like focusing on a tiny part of your picture to set the right brightness. If that part is in the middle, it's even better. If not, you can still do it by aiming your focus at that spot and locking the brightness. It works well when the background is much brighter or darker.

If you focus on a bright or dark spot, your picture might be too dark or too bright. To fix this, you can adjust a setting for better results. But if you focus on something in the middle with a bright sky or a colored wall around it, you'll get a good picture. Other things around the spot stay the same as how bright the picture is. It differs from another mode that looks at a bigger area to set the brightness.

Using Spot Metering

Matrix and Center-weighted metering are simple to use and have only a few settings to think about. They change based on exposure adjustments and a setting called Custom Setting b4: Fine-Tune Optimal Exposure. Spot metering is different and lets you choose where to measure the exposure. Here are some things to think about:

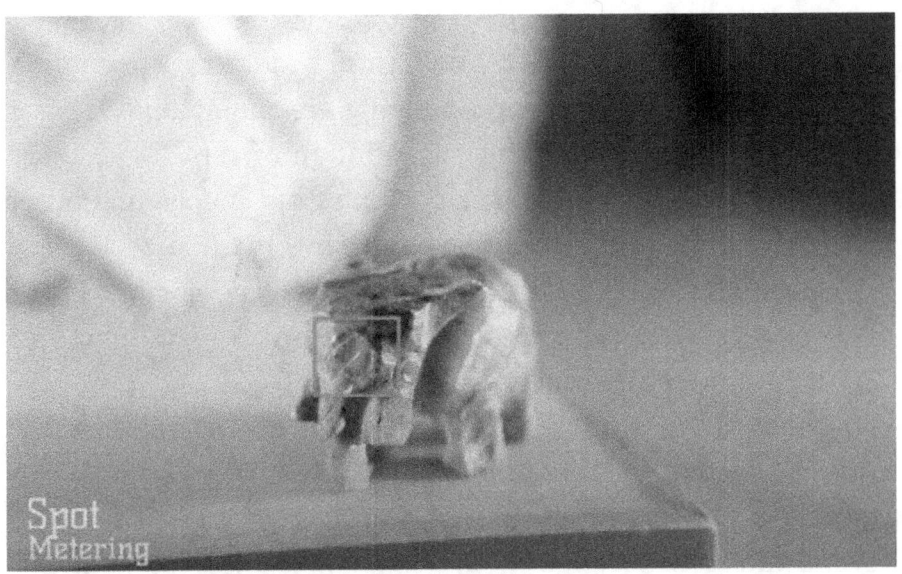

Moving the spot: You can't move the metering spot directly. It uses the same spot where your camera is currently focused. To change the spot, you must use an AF-area mode to adjust the focus area. Most modes work for this, except Auto-area AF. In that mode, the center focus point is always used for metering, and you can't change it.

Choosing a compatible AF-area mode: Use the "i" menu to change the focus area while taking pictures. The available focus areas depend on the focus mode you're using. You can pick any focus point from the areas shown on the screen.

- **AF-S focus mode:** Choose how the camera focuses: Exact AF, One Point AF, Big Area AF (Small), or Big Area AF (Large). (Please note: You can't use Dynamic Area AF.)
- **AF-C focus mode:** You can choose how the camera focuses: on one point, a moving area, a small area, or a large area. But you can't use Pinpoint focus.
- **Manual focus mode:** You can only choose one point at a time. Remember, when using manual focus, the camera won't automatically focus. The focus point's position is only used for the electronic rangefinder and Spot metering functions.

Wrap-around: You can use the buttons on the sub-selector or multi-selector to move the focus point on the screen. It can also move the metering spot. The focus point will only go beyond the screen's edges if you've enabled focus point wrap-around in Custom Setting a8.

When using Auto-area AF: If you choose Auto-area AF, the camera will use the center focus point even if it picks a different point to focus on. It is a good thing because, in this mode, you will know the focus spot once you press the shutter halfway. Spot metering works best when you're not using Auto-area AF, but it works differently.

Reminder: When the focus point moves, the spot metering point moves, too. If you're using Dynamic-area AF and continuous autofocus (AF-C), the camera might change the focus point you picked and focus on the nearby points instead. The metering area will do the same thing.

Highlight-weighted Metering

In this mode, the camera looks at your whole picture to decide how to set the exposure, similar to the Matrix mode. Even though its symbol looks like the Spot mode, it's not the same. In this mode, the camera's processors find the bright parts of your picture and set the exposure to avoid making them too bright. The other parts of the picture are less important. This mode is good for pictures where the bright parts cover a big area. It might have been useful for the flamingo picture, but it's even better for pictures with big, bright areas.

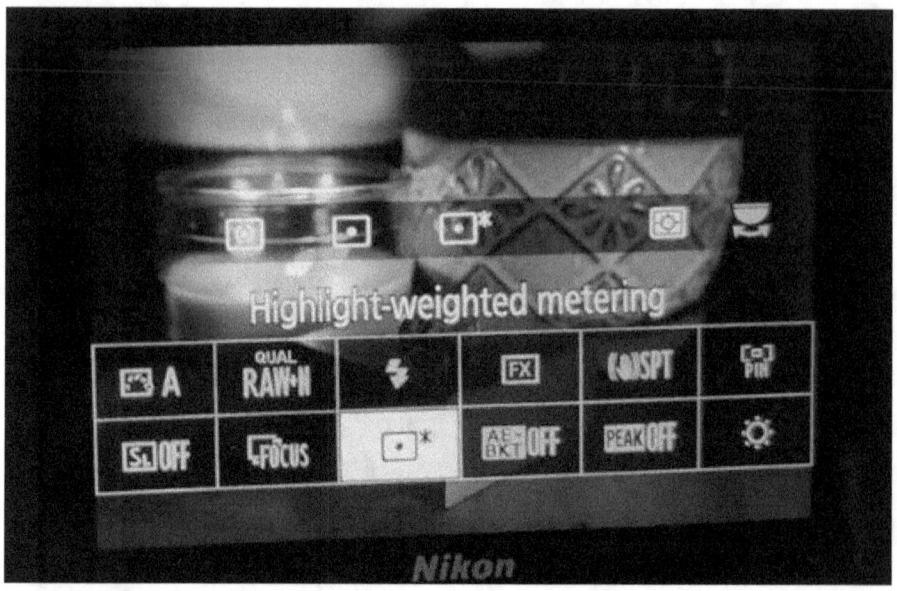

If you're taking pictures of performers on a lit-up stage during a concert or play, the camera can figure out the right brightness for the performers while ignoring the dark parts around them. You can choose to measure the brightness in Spot mode, where you put a small measuring point on the dancer's face or shirt. Or you can use Highlight-weighted metering, which lets the camera decide how bright the performer should be. The results will be similar depending on how well you choose the measuring spot and how good the camera is at telling the performer from the background. I use Spot metering when the area I want to measure is clear and Highlight-weighted metering when there are different levels of brightness I want to keep, like in the picture of Billy Zoom from the punk band X.

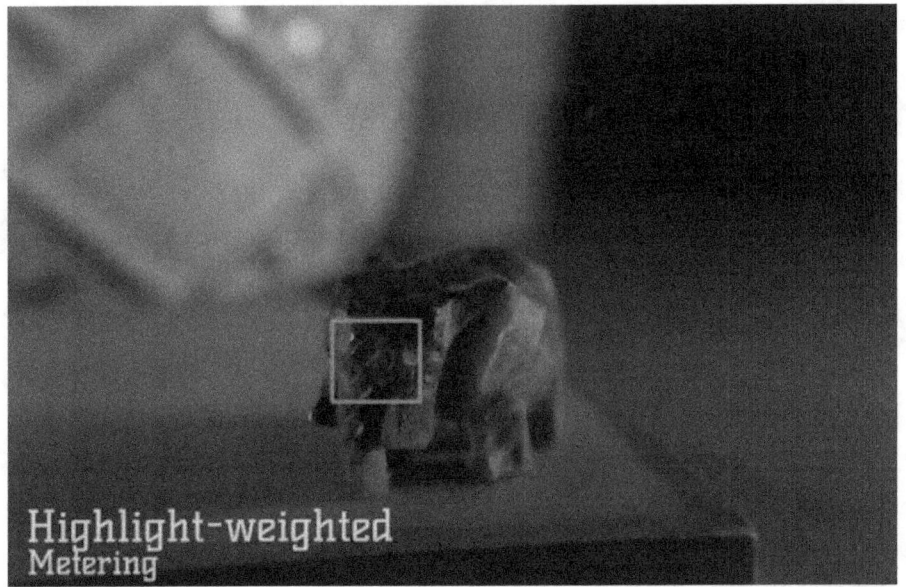

CHAPTER 5: CAPTURING VIDEO

Quick Start Checklist

Here are some tips to help you improve at making movies and improving your video work. Some of these points relate to things you've already learned about taking photos, while others are specific to making movies. Even if you're skimming through this chapter for now and planning to return after exploring movie-making, read this section before you start working on your big documentary or feature film.

Also, you can capture high-quality still photos while recording a video. Press the shutter button fully, and you'll get a cropped photo matching the movie's aspect ratio. It won't interrupt your video recording. The picture will have the same quality as your movie, whether in HD or 4K mode, with images of 1920 × 1080 (2MP) for HD and 3840 × 2160 (8MP) for 4K.

If you pick Continuous release mode, the camera will take only one photo each time you press the button while recording a video. This way, you can take up to 50 shots with it.

No flash: You can take pictures while recording a video but can't use the flash when the camera is set to Movie mode.

Exposure compensation: In movies, you can adjust the brightness slightly using exposure compensation. You can make it brighter or darker in small steps. For movies, you can change it by 3 steps; each step is smaller than usual. But for photos, you can change it in 5 steps.

Size matters: Movies can be as big as 4GB (the file size) and as long as 29 minutes and 59 seconds. A movie might have up to 8 parts, each 4GB, based on how you set the quality. The number of parts and their lengths depend on those settings. Your memory card's speed and space also limit things. When using slow-motion, movies can be up to three minutes long.

Use the right card: Use a fast memory card like XQD or CFexpress for best results. If you use a slower card, your recording might stop quickly, especially for high-quality videos. You need a card that can handle different transfer rates, like 28 Mbps for full HD, 56 Mbps for High Quality, and 144 Mbps for 4K videos. Make sure the card has at least 32GB capacity.

I personally prefer 128GB and 256GB CFexpress cards, like the Sony G series and ProGrade. They have fast write speeds of around 1400–1480 Mbps and can handle 4K shooting well. Remember, the camera can't shoot a continuous movie for more than 29 minutes, but you can start the next clip immediately if you have enough space on the card and battery power.

Carry extra cards: You're probably used to taking still photos. It's easy to know how much space you've used on your memory card and how much is left by looking at the indicator on the screen. But when shooting videos, it's a bit different. Even though the camera shows how much space you have left for a video, it can sometimes be clearer how much space is left on your memory card. To be sure, you must go to the Movie Shooting menu to check. Bringing more memory cards than you'll need is a good idea.

Add an external mic: For the best sound quality and to avoid picking up the autofocus or zoom motor sound, get an external stereo mi.

Minimize zooming: Using the zoom to make faraway things look closer is nice, but be careful. If you're not using an extra microphone, the zoom noise might be heard while watching the video. Moving the zoom a lot can bother people who watch your videos. Also, the picture will look better if you use digital zoom. So, if you care about how the video looks, avoid using digital zoom, especially if you're trying to record something important that's far away.

Use a fully charged battery: AA new battery lets you record for around 85 minutes in regular temperatures (not winter), but this might be less if you change the focus a lot. Each recording can be up to 29 minutes long, though.

Keep it cool: The video quality can worsen if the camera's sensor gets hot. So, make sure to keep the camera in a cool spot. On hot days, the sensor can heat up faster than normal. If it gets too hot, the camera will stop recording and turn off after about five seconds. Wait for it to cool down before using it again.

Press the Movie button: You don't need to keep holding it. Just press it again to stop recording.

Lean, Mean, Movie Machine

The Z7 II camera is the best video cameras ever made by the company that first introduced video capabilities in a camera with interchangeable lenses, starting with the Nikon D90 in 2008. Back then, the D90 could only record simple movies with no color using manual focus at a fixed rate of 24 frames per second. It could record up to five minutes in 1280 × 720p resolution, standard HD. If you lowered the quality to 640 × 424 or 320 × 216, you could record longer clips, up to 20 minutes.

Your camera has amazing features that were only a dream for people using video camcorders a few years ago. But for now, if you want a quick overview, look at this list.

Full HD capture: You can make clear and detailed videos with a resolution of 1920 × 1080. You can record them at speeds like 60, 30, 25, or 24 frames per second. If you want to zoom in a bit for your videos using a specific part of the camera, you can also pick faster frame rates like 120/100 frames per second or 50 frames per second. I'll tell you more about frame rates and stuff like that later on.

4K video capture: You can record clear videos in Ultra-High Definition (UHD), which has a resolution of 3840 × 2160. This camera can capture videos at different rates: 30, 25, and 24 frames per second. There would be an update for the camera that allowed it to capture even higher quality 4K videos at 60 frames per second, but only when using a specific mode. This mode is necessary for the 60 frames per second recording, and the camera keeps the 4K video it records inside itself and can't send it to another device.

Slow-motion video: You can record videos in really clear quality, like the ones you see on TV, for up to three minutes. You can also make the videos playback in slow motion, 4 or 5 times slower. It can help look closely at things like your golf swing or capture scenes like lifeguards running in slow motion, similar to Baywatch.

Zebra stripe highlight display: If parts of the picture are too bright (more than you want), you can use a special pattern to show those areas.

Phase-detection AF: Having a camera that can quickly and smoothly focus while recording videos is important. The camera uses special pixels, and it works for both high-quality 4K videos and regular HD videos. If you prefer to focus manually, there's a feature called Focus Peaking that outlines objects in focus with colored lines on the screen.

IBIS and Electronic VR: Take smooth handheld videos without needing a SteadyCam. It is possible because of the camera's built-in technology that helps counteract shaky movement and a special mode that reduces blurriness caused by the camera moving.

Easy AF point placement: Use the touch screen or the small joystick to find the right focus point while taking a picture.

Output to an external video recorder: Your camera works well with a cheaper external monitor called Atomos Ninja V ($600). It can send clear video to the monitor through an HDMI port. You can save your videos on another device and watch them on a big, bright screen.

10-bit N-log capture: N-log is a special setting that helps cameras record videos with many shades of light and color. It initially makes the video look plain, but this helps keep all the details. Later, when editing the video, you can make it look nice by adjusting the colors and brightness. Nikon even has a feature called "View Assist" that lets you see a better version of the video on the camera before you edit it.

Other output options: Besides capturing N-log, you can send 10-bit HLG HDR video to an external recorder. If you pay $199 (plus shipping), you can have Nikon update your camera's firmware to allow you to send 12-bit line-skipped 4K Raw video to an external recorder using ProRes Raw or Blackmagic Raw.

Timecode: Your video can have special codes that help match up, record, and find different parts. You can set different things for taking pictures and making videos. It lets your camera work the way you want for each mode.

Capturing Video

In the Movie Shooting menus, you can pick from choices explained in Chapter 11, including a description of the different options for each. I won't repeat the same things. Many of these choices are similar to the ones for taking pictures in the Photo Shooting menu.

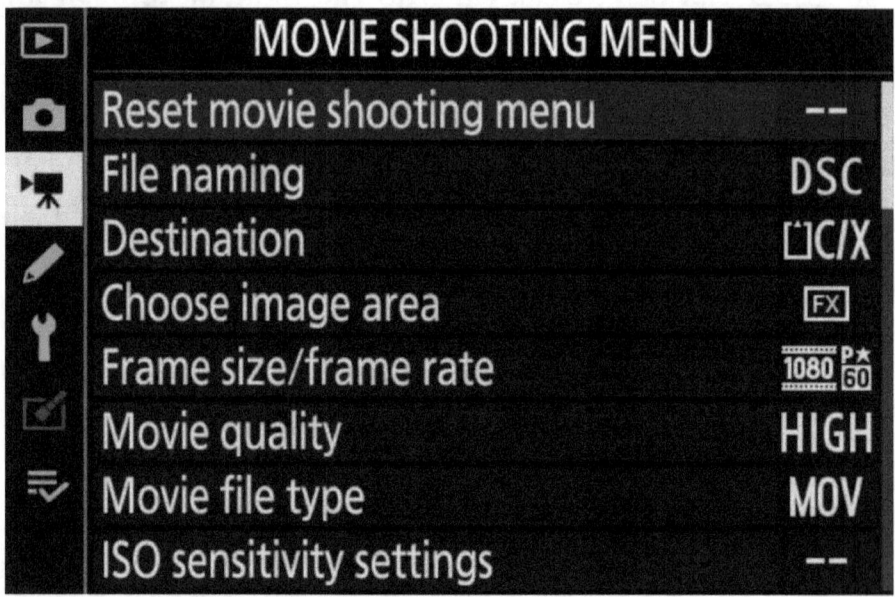

File Naming: When naming your movie files, I suggest picking another word to replace the default letters in Movie mode. I usually use NZ7 for pictures and MOV for videos. Follow the same rules and guidelines as the File Naming section in the Photo Shooting menu.

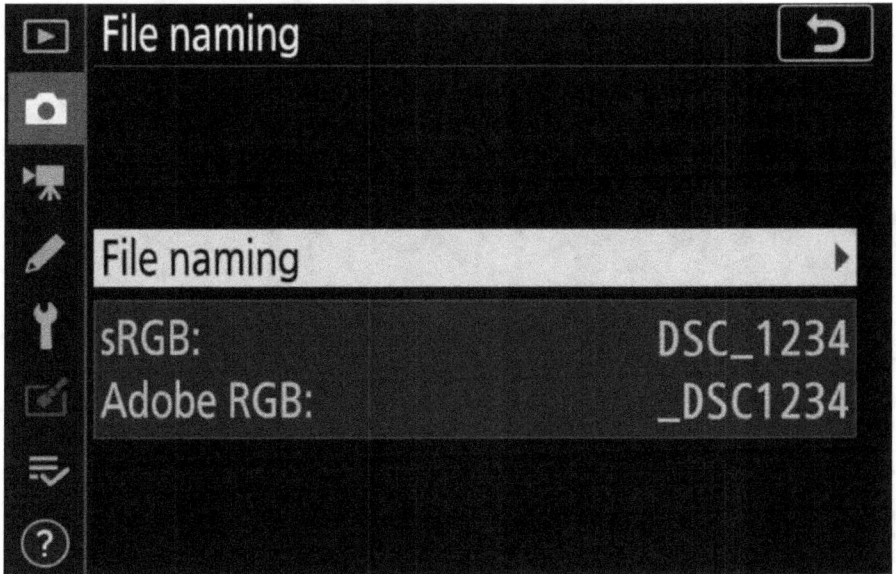

Destination: You can choose which memory card slot to save videos. You can pick a different card for videos than the one you set as the main and backup slots in the Photo Shooting menu. The app shows how much video storage time is left when you choose.

Image Area: This setting decides how much of the picture is captured when making videos. You can choose from different choices.

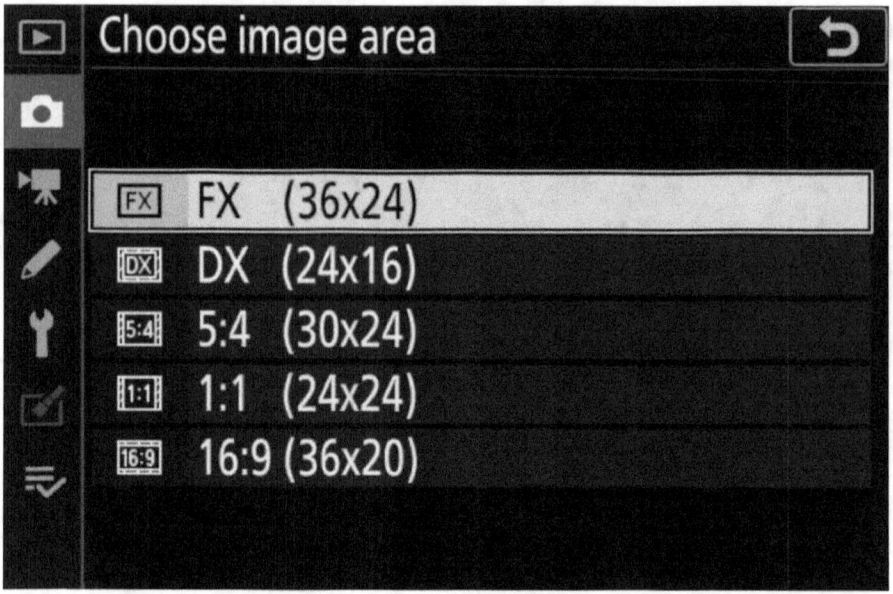

- **Choose Image Area:** This camera has two ways to capture movies: FX and DX. These let you record videos using either a wider or more cropped view. The DX mode creates a movie resembling an HDTV screen, while the FX mode captures a wider scene. The camera doesn't put a visible border around the cropped DX area; it enlarges the cropped video to fill the screen. The normal FX view is also shown.

Frame Size/Frame Rate: Here, you can choose 10 different video styles for regular movies. There are also three extra choices for videos that play in slow motion. The regular options provide high-quality videos: 4K resolution (3840 × 2160) at different speeds (30/25/24 frames per second). You can also have Full HD (1920 × 1080) at different speeds (60/50/30/25/24 frames per second) or Standard HD (1280 × 720) at different speeds (60/50 frames per second). The faster and slower speeds are used in different parts of the world depending on the video systems they use.

Movie Quality: Choose between High Quality or Normal Quality. Your decision impacts how clear and detailed your image will be, the maximum amount of data your video can have, and how long your recorded movies can be. If you have fast memory cards and plan to watch your video on larger screens, it's better to go for High Quality. Remember that you can only shoot 4K video using High Quality. If you've chosen to capture in UHD (4K), the option for Movie Quality will be unavailable. Using video editing software, you can often change a video to a lower-quality version.

Movie File Type: You can pick either MOV or MP4 files. MOV works best on Macs, but it also works on Windows. MP4 is a common format that works on both Macs and PCs. Video-editing software can change between them easily.

ISO Sensitivity Settings (for Movies): Like the ISO settings in the Photo Shooting menu, this option lets you pick a specific ISO value when using Manual mode. It gives you more control over the sensitivity of your camera's sensor, allowing you to adjust it between ISO 100 and ISO 25600, with some higher options. The camera automatically adjusts the ISO for videos taken in specific exposure modes. But if you're using Manual mode for videos and want the camera to handle the ISO, you can turn on Auto ISO and set the maximum ISO value it will use.

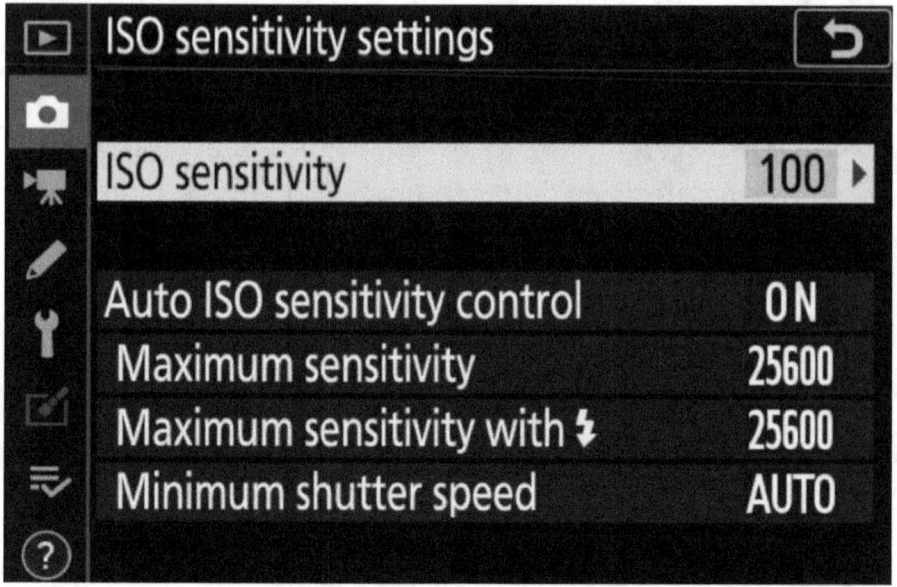

Next, there's something called "White Balance." It affects the color tone of your videos. You can choose different settings to ensure your videos' colors look accurate.

- **Same As Photo Settings:** The camera will use the white balance setting you picked in the Photo Shooting menu.
- **Any of the other white balance options:** This choice affects only videos. It's hard to change the white balance for videos, so it's best to pick a white balance option from this menu or use Auto. I typically use the same white balance as I do for photos.

Set Picture Control: You can use the same settings as in the photo or set a different Picture Control just for videos. The steps to pick and change the Picture Control are the same.

One special option is the Flat Picture Control, which dulls the image. It might seem odd, but it's useful because it captures more details in the bright and dark areas of the video. It lets you make precise adjustments to the video's colors and appearance when editing, like changing contrast, colors, and more. It is beneficial with flat-looking images from the Flat Picture Control or N-log gamma.

Manage Picture Control: This section has options like Save/Edit, Rename, Delete, and Load/Save. These work just like the similar controls in the Photo Shooting menu. You can copy, edit, save, rename, or delete a Picture Control style and get a Picture Control from a memory card.

Active D-Lighting: You can pick settings like "Same as Photo," "Extra High," "High," "Normal," "Low," or "Off."

High ISO NR: During filming movies, there's no need for long camera exposures. So, the Movie Shooting menu has a High ISO Noise Reduction section. You can choose from options like High, Normal, Low, or Off to control how much noise reduction is applied to the video.

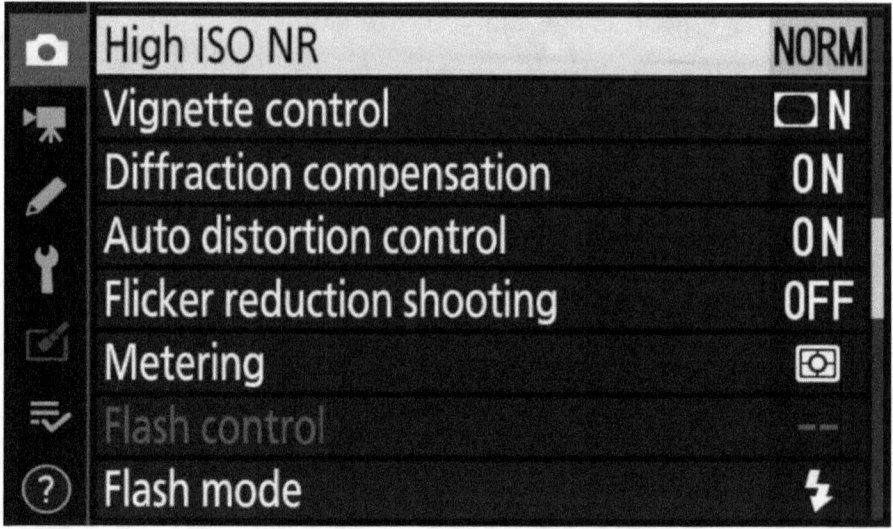

Vignette Control/Diffraction Compensation/Auto Distortion Control: All three work the same way when taking still photos.

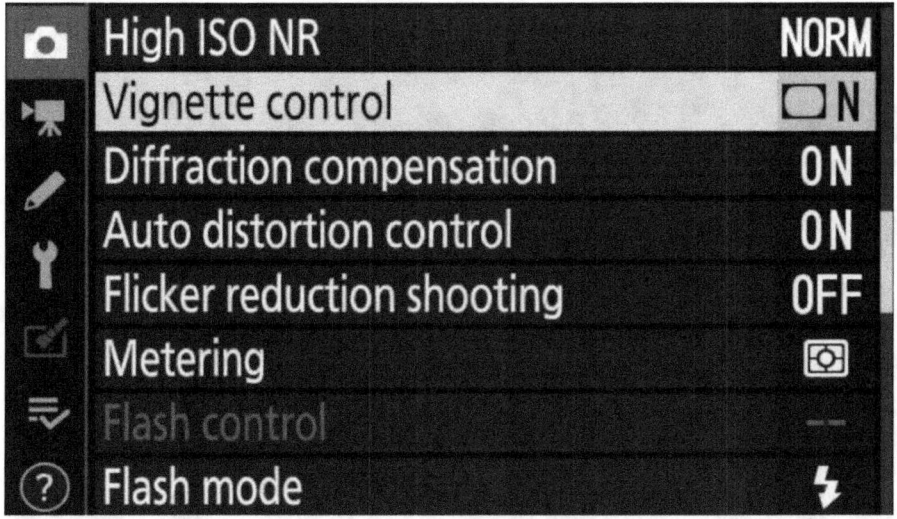

Flicker Reduction: Pick "Auto" or choose between 50Hz and 60Hz.

Metering: You can only use Matrix, Center-weighted, and Highlight-weighted metering, but Spot metering isn't an option in Movie mode.

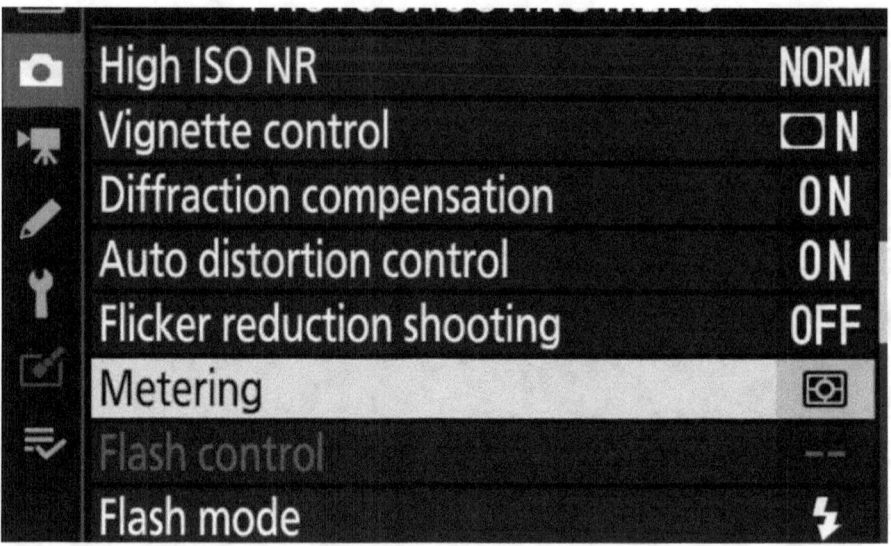

Focus Mode: In Movie mode, there's a new focus mode called Full-time AF (AF-F). Unlike other modes, you don't have to press any buttons to use it. It stays active all the time while you're shooting a video. Although it uses more power, it helps the camera focus quickly when you start recording.

AF-Area Mode: You can only use Single-point AF, Wide-area AF (Small), Wide-area AF (Large), and Auto-area AF. You can't use Pinpoint AF in Movie mode.

Vibration Reduction: This option lets you control how the camera's built-in stabilization works. You can pick from options like matching photo settings, normal mode, sports mode, or turning it off completely.

Electronic VR: This kind of electronic image stabilization doesn't move the camera's insides like IBIS. Instead, it trims the video and shifts it around to counteract some of the camera's movement. But it won't work with certain video settings. You'll see a waving hand on the screen when this is on. The highest sensitivity for videos is set at ISO 25,600. Remember, because of the trimming, the view angle narrows, making things seem more zoomed in.

Microphone Sensitivity: This entry gives you three choices for controlling the microphone. You can pick Auto Sensitivity, where the device adjusts the recording level for you, or Manual Sensitivity, where you can adjust the level yourself using a volume meter on the screen. You can also turn the microphone off if you're recording quiet video, using another recording source, or adding sound later.

Attenuator: Turn on this option to reduce noise from the background when recording videos in noisy places.

Frequency Response: Choose the Wide Range option to capture many different sounds, or pick Vocal Range for the best recording of voices.

Wind Noise Reduction: When the wind blows onto your microphone, it can be annoying. This setting helps to lessen the sound of the wind (but it might also change how other sounds come through, so be cautious). It works only for the microphones that are already in your device. If you're using an external microphone like the Nikon ME-1, it might have its switch to reduce wind noise.

Headphone Volume: You can choose how loud the sound is, from 1 being quiet to 30 being loud. The usual level is 15.

Timecodes: We won't go into detailed topics like advanced video editing or software like Photoshop. Timecodes are advanced, and those who know how to use them won't need my instructions. But Nikon cameras with interchangeable lenses now have a cool new feature: timecodes. These are like precise time markers in videos. They show the hour, minute, second, and even the frame of a video. It helps match up different parts of the video and the audio. The timecode system even has a way to handle small adjustments in frame rates so the video matches the real-time correctly.

Time-Lapse Movie: This is like using a camera's timer to take pictures, but it's for videos. You find it in the picture-taking settings, not the video settings. It makes a quiet, fast-motion video using the settings you picked for videos.

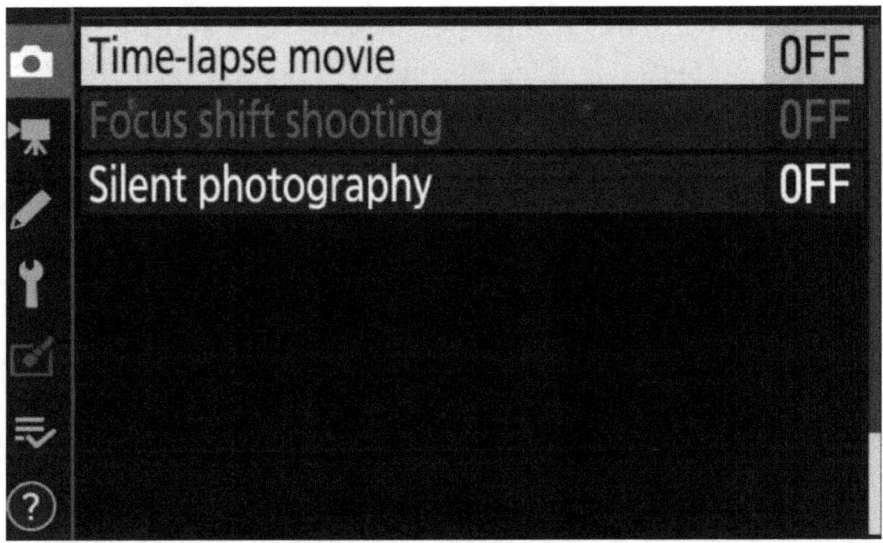

Slow-Motion Movies

Slow-motion video is a cool new thing that lets you make your videos play slower by 4 or 5 times. It is excellent for looking closely at movements or making videos with superheroes or lifeguards that move fast.

In the settings for making videos, you can choose to make the video size 1920 × 1080, and then you can pick either 30/25 frames per second times 4 for slow motion or 24 frames per second times 5 for slow motion. If you're in a place that uses PAL format, you can choose 25 frames per second times 4 or 24 frames per second times 5 for slow motion instead.

When you use the slow-motion mode on the camera, it records videos that look normal but playback slower. It records at a faster speed (120/100 frames per second) for a short time (up to three minutes). Watching this video at regular speed (30/25 frames per second) takes longer to play. For example, a three-minute video can become 12 minutes when watched at regular speed or even 15 minutes if watched at a slower speed (24 fps). This mode is helpful for studying your golf swing or making movies with a slow-motion effect. While it might seem like a limitation that you can only record for three minutes, think about how often you want to watch 12 to 15 minutes of slow-motion footage.

Shooting Your Movie

Now, it's time to start recording your video. Just follow these steps:

1. Plug in the microphone. If you're using an external microphone with a 3.5mm plug, attach it to the microphone jack on the camera's left side.
2. Pick a mode for how the camera adjusts to light. You can choose from Program, Shutter-priority, Aperture-priority, or Manual. The camera uses sensor readings to decide how to set the exposure.
3. Adjust the exposure settings. What you can adjust depends on the mode you pick:
   - **Program/Shutter-priority:** Use the EV button to brighten or darken the image. The camera chooses the shutter speed and ISO.

- **Aperture-priority:** Change the f/stop and adjust brightness with the EV button. The camera selects the shutter speed and ISO.
- **Manual:** Use the main dial to set the shutter speed (how fast the camera takes the picture) and the sub-dial for the aperture (how much light comes in). You can change ISO sensitivity by pressing the ISO button and turning the main dial.

4. To start recording a movie, switch the Photo/Movie switch to the Movie position.
5. Use the AF/MF switch on the camera to select whether the camera focuses automatically or manually. Then, choose AF-S or AF-F and pick where you want the camera to focus.
6. In the Movie Shooting menu, you can use the Microphone Sensitivity setting to control how loud the audio is in your recording. You can let the camera automatically set the volume or adjust it manually using the audio meter at the bottom of the screen. If you want a silent recording, like if you plan to add voice or music later, you can turn off the audio.
7. Press the red movie recording button to start recording. Press it again to stop. The screen will show what you're recording. If you're using the viewfinder instead of the screen, you can press the DISP button to change how much info is on the screen.

8. You can't use the camera flash while recording a movie, but you can use the LED movie light on the Nikon SB-500 unit.

CONCLUSION

Remember, photography is all about expressing yourself and capturing special moments. With your newfound knowledge, you're ready to unleash your creativity and capture stunning photos and videos like never before. Don't hesitate to experiment, try new things, and have fun with your camera.

Whether you're taking breathtaking landscapes, capturing candid portraits, or shooting amazing videos, the Nikon Z7 II is your tool to tell stories and make memories.

Keep exploring, keep learning, and keep shooting. The world is your canvas, and your Nikon Z7 II is your paintbrush. Happy photographing!

www.ingramcontent.com/pod-product-compliance
Lightning Source LLC
Chambersburg PA
CBHW062352290526
45794CB00005B/2199